PRAISE FOR
HOW TO HUNT GHOSTS

"Warren's book *How to Hunt Ghosts* is a rare find. The majority of books on ghosts simply list incidents and locations of hauntings, but this book provides you with the information to go out and find them for yourself. Many of the tools needed can be found at home or bought cheaply. The author's enthusiasm for his subject shines through. I'm sure this book will persuade many a sedentary armchair ghost hunter to get up out of his chair and go out hunting. I read a lot of books and few impress me. This one did!"

—Natalie Osborne-Thomason,
author of *The Ghost-Hunting Casebook*

"*How to Hunt Ghosts* is a straightforward, no-nonsense guide for those who want to seek out spirits and understand hauntings in both practice and theory. From defining those bumps in the night to describing the equipment with which to document paranormal encounters, author Joshua Warren provides the ever-curious ghostbuster with a functional manual for success."

—Patricia Telesco, author of *Ghosts, Spirits and Hauntings*

"I was intrigued by Joshua Warren's analytical approach to the phenomena of ghosts and ghost hunting. Everyone interested in this subject will find this book a fascinating read."

—Nancy Roberts, author of *Haunted Houses*

"*How to Hunt Ghosts* is a well-written and informative book. It proves the existence of the spiritual world, a world that should be taken very seriously."

—Kathleen Keating, author of *Torn Sky*

"A fascinating work by a long-time student of psychic phenomena who is much respected and consulted. His latest work takes an in-depth look at all types of ghostly activity, and it deserves the widest possible readership."

—Peter Underwood, author of *Borley Postscript*
and President of The Ghost Club Society

HOW TO HUNT
GHOSTS

A PRACTICAL GUIDE

Joshua P. Warren

A Fireside Book
Published by Simon & Schuster
New York London Toronto Sydney Singapore

FIRESIDE
Rockefeller Center
1230 Avenue of the Americas
New York, NY 10020

For information about special discounts for bulk purchases,
please contact Simon & Schuster Special Sales:
1-800-456-6798 or business@simonandschuster.com

Designed by Jaime Putorti

Manufactured in the United States of America

1   3   5   7   9   10   8   6   4   2

Library of Congress Cataloging-in-Publication Data
Warren, Joshua P.
  How to hunt ghosts: a practical guide / Joshua P. Warren.
      p. cm.
  "A Fireside book."
  Includes bibliographical references (p.) and index.
    1. Ghosts. I. Title.

BF1471.W37 2003
133.1–dc21   2003042465

ISBN   0-7432-3493-6 (pbk.)

I dedicate this book to:

My warm and loving family, who have always given me infinite support . . .

Craig Madison and Dave Tomsky of the Grove Park Inn, who took a chance with a kid . . .

The L.E.M.U.R. Team, for so many great friends and spine-tingling adventures . . .

And Bill Forstchen, who swept down from the sky and changed everything . . .

Thank you.
JPW

CONTENTS

INTRODUCTION

Ghosts are real. By the time you've finished reading this book, you will know how to find and study them effectively. Whether you seek to document the presence of spirits, gain greater understanding of the "other side," or clear a location of ghostly activity, you will find assistance in this guide. I have been an active paranormal investigator for more than a decade, and in that time I've visited hundreds of "haunted" locations and interviewed thousands of people. Using scientific data gathering and journalistic techniques, I've come to understand spiritual activity on a realistic scale. Through this manual, I share my experience with you.

At its core, spiritual activity conjures up complex and philosophical issues. After all, we're often dealing with another facet of life and death. The ultimate meaning of life, its origin and its destiny, is perhaps mankind's greatest scientific enigma. With our current technology, we cannot expect to solve this mystery here. However, even though we cannot conclusively identify the role of ghosts in the great scheme of life, we *can* use science to document their influence on the environment.

We must begin by defining a ghost. Why does a ghost appear? What does it mean if you encounter one? We will explore theories that may help explain how a ghost is formed. Then, we will apply this knowledge—using it in connection with affordable instruments and easy techniques to study supernatural activity. Despite what you've seen in the movies, there is no such thing as a "ghost meter," a device that registers a specific phantasmal body. The creation of such an instrument would be dependent upon a complete understanding of a ghost's unique physical makeup, an understanding that to date does not exist. However, spirits create changes in the normal environment. It is by documenting those changes that we may indirectly pinpoint ghosts. The method has been likened to searching for a person on a beach. We are not necessarily looking for the individual, but instead, his or her footprints in the sand. If we find footprints, we can then speculate as to their origin. Were these impressions merely a trick of the water on the beach? Were they caused by a human? Can we be certain they are human prints? It is therefore necessary for a ghost hunter to possess a scrutinizing mind. You must rule out all conventional explanations before resorting to a supernatural one.

Researching the unexplained is largely a process of elimination. When you are not absolutely sure what you seek, how do you know when you find it? The best method is to weed out all ordinary possibilities. What remains is most likely the product of a phenomenon still misunderstood by current science.

Though the idea of a spiritual realm has far-reaching implications, the purpose of this guide is to provide clear, concise instructions on gaining research results. It is the simplest and most complete introduction to the world of practical spiritual study. Whether you seek to start a full-time research team or simply answer a few of your personal questions, you can tailor the included information to suit your specific needs.

Since, with each passing day, we grow closer to solving the mysteries of the universe, the information contained here may have limited potency. As we learn more about the spirit realm, our ways of studying it will surely develop and mature. However, such changes may never occur unless we first explore using the most basic techniques.

Step-by-step, you will learn how to study ghostly activity in the most elementary ways. What you learn should be applied to new, original, and innovative means of breaching the gap between physical and spiritual reality. If you're serious about studying and understanding ghosts, this is the book for you.

PART ONE:

UNDERSTANDING GHOSTS

WHAT IS A GHOST?

Also called spirits, phantoms, wraiths, visions, shades, specters, haints, and apparitions, we can loosely define a ghost as *some paranormal aspect of the physical form and/or mental presence that appears to exist apart from the original physical form.* The word *appears* is integral to the definition. Most ghostly encounters are evaluated by the five physical senses alone. This makes most information about ghosts *subjective* (dependent upon an observer's limited perception). One must be careful about drawing conclusions based upon subjective evidence. *Objective* evidence (dependent upon external, unbiased measurement, equally obtainable by all) is the pillar of scientific knowledge. Don't jump to conclusions based on subjective data. If you don't rule out the conventional, someone else will. Then, you look foolish.

You and I might never agree on the taste of a chocolate bar. What I consider a pleasurable taste might send you gagging. And so whose perception of the candy bar is correct? Does the chocolate taste good or bad? How can I say that my tongue has priority over yours, or vice versa? I could say that most people agree with me, but that still doesn't mean I'm inherently correct. There was a time when most people in the United States believed slavery was okay. However, the perception of the majority can change over time. The taste of a food is an example of subjective information. Its value is limited by someone's unique interpretation.

On the other hand, if we find a set of scales and agree upon its accuracy, we suddenly have mutual faith in this independent tool. Though our sensory perspectives are unique, the scales give us a common and definite standard by which to document reality. For instance, if we place the candy bar on the scales, it should be virtually impossible for us to disagree on its weight. This is an example of objective evidence. It is based on external measurement, and should be equally obtainable by all. The scientific method is founded on using objective evidence to establish a set of facts about any given phenomenon. Though this is the best way to conduct true science, it too has its faults. Information gathered in this way is only as valid as the tools and procedures used to gain it.

The task of defining a ghost is somewhat complicated because it can blur the line between a subjective experience and an objective event. Defining a ghost in words is one thing. But defining a ghost in reality is a bit more difficult. What exactly *qualifies* as "ghostly"? How about a light in the kitchen that switches itself on and off at random? Is that the product of a ghost? Is it the work of a physically dead human? Or is it the product of something else entirely, maybe something as simple as a faulty switch? How about an isolated patch of icy air, mysteriously moving about in an otherwise sweltering room? Is this some aspect of a human spirit? Or is it some rare and bizarre quirk in the atmospheric condition? Any of these events, by itself, may or may not be considered ghostly. But what if, on the other hand, that light blinks in a kitchen where your dead grandmother used to spend her day? Or what if that frigid patch of air floats in a room where your brother killed himself? Suddenly, do these events take on new possible meaning?

When primitive man first watched bits of iron lurch at magnets, surely it was considered ghostly. But ghostly activity is not always caused by a ghost. Likewise, a ghost does not always cause ghostly activity. Lots of spectral manifestations surround us each day, hidden in realms outside of naked human perception. A sharp mind is necessary to process all possibilities.

Webster's defines a ghost as "a disembodied human spirit." But that definition is far too narrow. Animals, as well as inanimate objects like ships and automobiles, also have ghosts. For example, *The Flying Dutchman* is a phantom vessel seen sailing the Cape of Good Hope for nearly two centuries. Almost every product of our living existence has been witnessed, at some point, as a spectral manifestation. Therefore, the possibilities are virtually endless.

Humans have been experiencing things they cannot explain for thousands of years. Most of the world's religions are based on the concept of a spiritual world, or an invisible dimension of existence that transcends our own. Even in the Holy Bible, chilling phantasmal encounters are described, like this passage from the Book of Job (4:15): "Then a spirit passed before my face; the hair of my flesh stood up."

However, despite the centuries of "ghostly encounters," such episodes are still considered unexplained. This is precisely why science is necessary. If we are to grow in our understanding, we must use the tools of our newest technologies to separate documented facts from rumor and myth. Despite what some may believe, there is indeed scientific evidence that ghostly manifestations are real. In this manual, we will focus on such evidence and the techniques for obtaining it. However, when it comes to investigating these matters, data alone cannot further our understanding. It is necessary for you, as an investigator, to interpret the data in relation to many historical, emotional, theoretical, and altogether psychological variables that might influence the meaning of your findings. Again, remember the example of the blinking kitchen light. The activity alone may seem insignificant, but in context with the location's history, the phenomenon may gain new meaning.

Ghost investigators often witness and document unexplainable events. However, proving that such activity is the product of a ghost is a different task. Witnessing a variety of bizarre activity is one matter; connecting the dots to prove such activity falls within the category of ghostly can be a different matter. Let me clarify:

I once investigated a haunted New Orleans mansion where heavy footsteps could be heard thumping up and down the wooden stairs at night. The owner of the home, a sweet, silver-haired woman, wasn't bothered by the activity. "You may call them a ghost, but to me they're just footsteps," she said. Indeed, she was right. And a recording of the phenomenon would be just as mundane—just footsteps. Even if they were the product of spiritual activity, documented with the best of today's technology, what would that really prove? Even when you successfully document an unexplained phenomenon, it may not prove anything about the source of the activity. Therefore, if you don't document the activity scientifically, you can forget *any* chance that your data will be taken seriously.

Sometimes, though rarely, a ghostly manifestation is obvious: an apparition walking across the room or communicating in some way. On the other hand, it is often more subtle, yet equally intriguing. A brief, disembodied whisper in your ear, or a soft, fleeting touch on your back, can be just as amazing as an inexplicable mist swirling down a hallway. Clearly, your interpretation of such events must be thoughtful. But, again, to interpret information correctly, one must approach from an unquestionably *objective* perspective.

Just because you're studying extraordinary activity, that doesn't mean you should abandon ordinary logic. Always remember the scientific principle known as Occam's Razor: In order to define a fact, assume as little as possible. The simplest explanation for a phenomenon is usually the correct one, and the less you take for granted, the more solid your conclusions will be. Throughout the text, I will reiterate the importance of always taking this approach.

The pursuit of ghostly activity is often called "paranormal" research. The prefix *para* means "beyond." Therefore, the term refers to studying *any* events beyond the realm of normal occurrences. But how do we define *normal*? Normal is any phenomenon that can be satisfactorily explained by known and widely accepted physical laws and standards. If an event cannot be fully explained by known scientific laws or information, it falls into the category of the paranormal. This label is much broader than that of ghosts, of course.

As a paranormal investigator, I never cease to be amazed by how little some people understand about what we do. When many people think of the paranormal, it conjures up popular images of ghosts, goblins, Sasquatches, UFOs, the Loch Ness Monster, and a handful of other esoteric subjects. However, those things represent only a sensational and highly fictionalized fraction of what we research. There was a time when lightning bolts were considered paranormal. There was a time when the sight of a jet streaming across the sky would have instilled panic and confusion in the casual observer. Obviously, everything we've ever learned about our world was at one time unknown. And yet there remain people who insist there's nothing left to be learned! Keep in mind the legend about Charles Duell, the head of the United States Patent Office in the late 1800s: He wanted to close the patent office in 1899 because he believed everything imaginable had already been invented.

As you can see, the world of paranormal research extends much further than a television special at Halloween. But the public tends to immediately associate a particular image with every occupation, and the world of the paranormal will always produce visions of things that go bump in the night. Why? Because people will always fear the unknown. And the unknown is what we study.

In his book *The Demon-Haunted World,* scientist Carl Sagan stated: "absence of evidence is not evidence of absence." There was no clear evidence of cellular or bacteria life until the microscope was invented. There was no clear evidence of the earth's magnetic field until the compass was created. Scientists believed coelacanths, a type of prehistoric fish, had been extinct for 65 million years, until one was pulled from South African waters in 1938. Prior to that fateful day, there was no evidence for the fish's existence. How many more "fateful days" lie in wait? In a literal sense, there is really no such thing as the supernatural or magical. Those are just glamorous names for a kind of natural technology we don't currently understand. At one time, a cigarette lighter would have been considered magical and supernatural. That doesn't mean it isn't real, though.

As you can see, the need for paranormal research is not only legitimate, but absolute. As such, all science is a form of paranormal research. Science is, in itself, a quest to learn—a quest to know the unknown; and yet, many conventional scientists call all paranormal pursuits "pseudoscience." Most mainstream sciences share one unavoidable fault: their essential need to limit themselves to studying activity of only a certain category. For example, a biologist is primarily occupied with living subjects, while an astronomer is principally concerned with bodies in space. After thousands of years of systematically searching for knowledge, the collective human experience has allowed us to create sciences that investigate the most frequent, common, and visible aspects of our life. However, there are still gaps. There are some gray areas between living and nonliving, plant and animal, reality and imagination. And within these realms occurs bizarre activity that no specific science is willing to officially adopt into its study. These activities sometimes seem to defy the laws according to which most of the universe functions. If the line between life and death were as clear as an equation, then there would be no controversy over abortion or life support machines. The issues attached to these two subjects directly challenge our ability to scientifically categorize something as seemingly simple and self-apparent as life and death. In fact, can we even prove that a human exists? We can document arms and legs, eyeballs and teeth, heartbeats and speech, and even personality. But is this all a human truly is? Or is there something more? Something not quite so apparent, yet perhaps most important of all?

When you're studying the unknown, how do you know if this activity should be examined by a geologist, a physicist, or a zoologist? A specialist in each of these fields might never make the effort to investigate a questionable phenomenon, eager to see if it will apply to his field. Though the curiosity might certainly be there, most scientists are busy enough researching the activity they already know about. However, if we are to truly expand the range of reality we're willing to study, someone must make the initial effort to examine these quirky phenomena and decide what field or fields might be best suited to further understand them. Therefore, a good paranormal researcher is someone who has a strong, general familiarity with most mainstream sciences. When documenting unknown phenomena, this gives the researcher the ability to better recognize which branches of science would be most useful in studying it.

Unfortunately, there are lots of illogical people running around out there calling themselves paranormal researchers. Indeed, they have every right to do so, considering that anyone with enough motivation can investigate an unknown subject. It somehow seems self-contradictory to obtain a "certification" to study the paranormal: How can you be certified to study an unknown subject? Therefore, in many cases, you end up with self-proclaimed researchers who don't approach any subject from a scientific standpoint. Some of them are clearly unstable people, or charlatans, who are more interested in promoting their beliefs than in collecting evidence. One rotten person can taint the image of the entire field. However, you must realize that *every* field has its wackos and incompetents. That means you should decide whether or not to trust a person based upon his or her track record. It's no different from choosing a surgeon. A smart person doesn't choose a surgeon based upon his proclamations alone. You need to see some examples of the doctor's work to feel satisfied.

Whether they officially title themselves or not, paranormal investigators are a crucial part of bringing the public's attention to matters worthy of further exploration. Doing scientific research is time-consuming and expensive. Big science doesn't want to spend time researching something unless the potential financial reward is substantial. Not all big-science research is a sure thing—e.g., AIDS research still hasn't resulted in a cure. No one wants to waste his or her time. Scientific progress is often directly related to money. The United States spent billions of dollars to create the atomic bomb on a deadline. If the money had not been available, you can rest assured that nuclear technology would not be where it is today. Look at the medical field. The development of new treatments and drugs is largely dependent upon the public's demand and willingness to fund it.

It is a mistake to forget that conventional scientists must pay bills just like you and me. Some of the most consistent and immediately profitable subjects take precedence over those that may not be profitable at all. That's why so many blatant, unexplainable phenomena are still around in the twenty-first century. One must be realistic. There is a limited amount of researchers, money, and time, yet there's a seemingly infinite amount of often inconsistent unexplainable activity. In fact, it seems clear that there are more phenomena that we *don't* scientifically understand than those that we do. Where did we come from? Where are we going? Is there a God? If so, who or what created God? What is the mind? How does it control the body? What are dreams? How is a lifetime of memories stored in a fist-sized hunk of flesh? What is the ultimate design and meaning of time? A conventional scientist might condescend toward paranormal research, but that scientist is as perplexed by these questions as anyone else. The implications of paranormal research are far larger than any handful of clichéd topics. However, for our purposes, we will focus on ghostly activity exclusively. As we'll discuss later, this mystery may be the most important one of all.

Ghost researchers are frequently called "parapsychologists." This term was coined because of psychologists studying extrasensory perception, or ESP. ESP is a general term, coined in the 1930s by well-known researcher J. B. Rhine of Duke University. It refers to using means other than the five ordinary physical senses—sight, hearing, taste, touch, and smell—to gain information. We know this more commonly as "psychic" phenomena. Since ghost research is indirectly related to ESP (as you will see), many parapsychologists have adopted it into their field of study as well. By the way, don't become a ghost hunter and then run around calling yourself a parapsychologist. There are laws that stipulate who can legally identify him- or herself as a psychologist of any kind.

The modern era of systematic ghost research began in England in the late 1800s. It was called psychical research. Throughout the history of ghost investigation, scientists have persisted in applying their own, specialized terminology to the field. This has caused some confusion among those trying to discuss the phenomena. What one person calls a phantom, another might call a demon. What one calls haunted, another might call a portal. With this book, I hope to cut through the confusion to establish some basic foundation for the activity. In many cases, it's premature to start dicing them up into terms. A classic example is how some people use the words *ghost* and *spirit* differently.

For our purposes, the terms *ghost* and *spirit* will be used interchangeably. Some people think of a spirit as being a uniquely human thing, an energy that carries your personality, whereas a ghost is any haunting vision of the past. However, it's not wise to play semantics at such a level. If you start categorizing things before you fully understand them, you're limiting your ability to connect two concepts freely. We will use the minimal amount of terminology necessary to gain a simple and strong understanding of a complex subject. Whether we call it a ghost, a spirit, a phantom, a wraith, a spook, or something else, it should still fit into our general definition of a ghost: *some paranormal aspect of the physical form and/or mental presence that appears to exist apart from the original physical form.*

Though the word *ghost* is used generously and impersonally, you must be mindful that ghosts may sometimes be conscious human beings in a different form. If so, we can assume that all the pride, emotions, and curiosities that accompany us in life, accompany us in a spiritual form. In life, the spectrum of human personalities is boundless. Why should it be different in an afterlife? We might call some conscious ghosts bad, or others good—just as we may call some living people bad or good. Whatever the case, it is ridiculous to fear all ghosts. If some ghosts are merely humans in a different form, you should view them humanely in your research.

It is also beneficial to keep in mind that if the ghosts you seek are humans in a different form, you can relate to them on a more realistic scale. Do all Texans wear big cowboy hats? Of course not; that's simply a stereotype. Do all ghosts hang out in graveyards or rattle chains? Of course not. Don't go looking for silly stereotypes and then become disappointed when you don't find them.

In keeping with our definition, a ghost can be the presence of something that was once conscious or nonconscious. For example, people see ghosts of humans and ghosts of automobiles. They see ghosts of horses *and* the stagecoach they pull. Basically, they see the ghosts of both living and nonliving things. So, what does this mean? How can we break it down from there? To get us started, I have divided ghostly activity into five basic categories, based upon both my own research and the work of others:

1. Entities
2. Imprints
3. Warps
4. Poltergeists
5. Naturals

Soon, we will explore each type of activity and how it may influence our perception of reality. However, before we explore such subjects, there is one topic that should be briefly addressed:

As I'm sure you've gathered, this book tackles scientific concepts. Such issues can be approached by examining evidence or scrutinizing laws of matter. This book does not address those specific concepts raised by religion. The reason there are so many religions is that one does not need evidence to form his or her religion. Religion is instead based on how one chooses to apply meaning to life. If evidence were a necessary foundation for religion, there would not be so many religions throughout the world. The issue would be greatly simplified: PROVE your views. But this is not what religion is about. Religion is about how you make personal sense of the chaos of life; science is about how you define the universe according to provable laws.

Despite what some may tell you, ghost research does not contradict religious integrity. There are many religions with conflicting views. To see life through religious eyes, one must usually choose and equip a system of predetermined beliefs. However, one desiring scientific knowledge does not *choose*, but instead *explores.* If a viewpoint, religious or otherwise, is correct and true, then it should stand up to any and all scrutiny and criticism. After all, the truth cannot be unseated. Therefore, it makes no sense to worry about acquiring new knowledge. If one's previous beliefs are true, research will only confirm this. If they are incorrect, though, they will crumble. If you seek to know truth in life, absorb all knowledge. Any institution, religious or otherwise, that commands you to limit your intake of scientific knowledge is afraid of its faults being exposed. An unscrupulous salesman will never tell you to look at his competition's selection. One offering the best deal will welcome the comparison, however. The best deal has nothing to fear.

There is a unique irony in how the public treats the idea of religion in relation to ghost research. Many religions are founded on the concept of an afterlife. One is told to believe in this afterlife based on faith alone. A need for faith implies that no concrete evidence is available. On the other hand, paranormal investigators have found evidence that may indicate we indeed *do* have an afterlife. Ironically, instead of seeing this information as beneficial, religions often find it threatening. Why must science and religion necessarily contradict each other? Is it possible the two are often addressing the same subjects, but from a different perspective? Many religions, especially Christianity, are founded on spiritual or otherwise paranormal activity.

ENTITIES

An entity is a ghost that appears to be conscious and often interactive. It is an active, individual personality. Though this definition can apply to some being *other* than a human, entities are most often humans or animals who have died. When most people think of a ghost, they think of an entity. These are the principal characters in most traditional ghost stories, and the majority of ghostly activity does indeed seem to be caused by entities. Our society has given us an informal idea that you are a combination of a body and soul. If this is correct, and the soul leaves the body at death, then an entity is most commonly viewed as this disembodied soul. But does this idea hold water? How can it be? What evidence do we have?

If it is true that a ghost is some remnant of a once-living creature, human or animal, then you are simply a ghost *with a body.* In other words, if a ghost can be something we leave behind, it is necessary for us to possess it before we die. We can therefore learn about some spiritual phenomena by studying the living physical body.

All matter, including the human body, can be better understood by breaking it down to its smallest particles. Matter breaks down into cells and molecules, then atoms, and finally electrical particles. Basic grammar-school science teaches us that electrons, protons, and neutrons bind the universe. Electrical charges are surrounded by magnetic fields, and magnetic fields can produce electrical charges. The two go hand-in-hand in the composition of nature. Together, charges and fields create electromagnetic energy—the essential hybrid of their interaction. Therefore, like all matter, our bodies are both surrounded and permeated by electromagnetic energy. These electromagnetic fields are generally called EMFs.

Our bodies are actually electrical machines. With each beat of our hearts, an electric pulse is released. Our brain waves, nervous system, muscular control, and most every other function of the body, operate according to electrical principles. Scientists can monitor and measure such energy with highly sensitive instruments like Josephson junctions and superconducting quantum interferometric devices (SQUIDs).

Many people don't realize that the body generates a magnetic field because metal objects don't stick to us. By the same token, we don't influence compass needles or "feel" the lines of force from a magnet. However, once again, EVERYTHING has a magnetic field. Recently, scientists at the University of Nijmegen in the Netherlands have been using this fact to cause tiny animals, such as frogs and spiders, to levitate. The creatures are placed into a small chamber, only inches in diameter. Then, they are subjected to an extraordinarily powerful magnetic field. They effortlessly rise and float, suspended in true, balanced levitation. It's similar to placing two magnets side by side with north facing north or south facing south. An invisible force field makes them oppose each other. An identical process could cause humans to float in the same way. However, the field necessary for human levitation would have to be far more powerful than any we've ever manufactured.

You can't make a paperclip stick to your forehead because the body's field is simply too subtle. Nonetheless, it's there. Even a piece of wood—seemingly as nonmagnetic as it gets—can be made to react to magnetism. Our energy fields may not be strong enough to readily manipulate objects around us, but in the presence of a large enough field, our bodies could become just as helpless as a thumbtack zipping across a table to smack a magnet. You should also note that when organisms are made to float by being subjected to such tremendous energy, it does not appear to harm them in any way.

In addition to these natural fields of electromagnetic energy, your body also carries static electrical charges. Of course, this is the same kind of electricity produced when you drag your socks across the carpet and touch a doorknob to receive a small shock. In fact, your body can carry thousands of volts of such energy. Some companies even manufacture toys that can operate from this electricity. One that comes to mind is the Human-Powered Light Bulb, distributed by the Copernicus company of Charlottesville, Virginia. It's a small bulb that illuminates when you touch it!

Your energy field basically follows the contours of your physical body. That means it looks just like you. It is, in essence, a three-dimensional energy mold of your physical form. Spiritualists talked about this field of energy long before there was scientific proof of its existence. They often call this field the "etheric body." If a camera could photograph the etheric body, and then remove the physical body from the picture, it might be feasible to obtain an image of your ghost. Of course, we're simply talking about an energy form that closely resembles your physical self. In fact, you might even consider it an additional, albeit invisible, layer of your body.

Kirlian photography is a controversial technique that some claim *can* photograph the etheric body (Illus. 1). This type of photography was explored by Russian researchers Semyon Davidovitch Kirlian and Valentina Kirliana in the early 1960s. Kirlian photos are made, basically, by passing a high voltage, low amperage current through an object while it's placed directly on a photographic plate. The current can also be given to the photographic plate, so that it travels through and into the subject. As the electricity passes through the negative, it creates a photographic image. Kirlian photos are most commonly taken of human hands or fingers. The developed prints show a fiery aura of light surrounding objects—more intense with living things than inanimate ones.

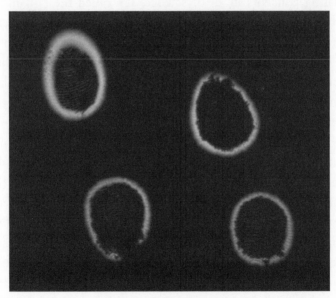

1. This Kirlian photograph shows coronas of energy around a subject's fingertips.
Photo courtesy Kirlianlab.com

This phenomenon may be the result of charging the etheric body with so much electricity that it becomes visible photographically. It's a way to document a pure coronal discharge. You'll learn more about this effect later, but it's a matter of charging an object with so much electricity that some leaks away. The manner in which this discharge occurs may represent qualities of the body's natural energy field.

Some critics claim the Kirlian effect is solely the product of moisture in the items. However, in many cases, a monk's or healer's aura can be enhanced if he or she prays or meditates. This seems to provide evidence that one's state of mind can alter the field of energy. These variances are often so extreme that slightly changing moisture levels alone, perhaps from sweating palms, could not cause them.

Kirlian photography also gives rise to one of the most fascinating concepts in all of science. It's called the "phantom leaf phenomenon." If one takes a Kirlian photograph of a leaf, the standard aura of light surrounds it. However, if the tip of the leaf is cut away, and the leaf is Kirlian photographed again, the tip will sometimes *still* develop (Illus. 2). It implies that even though the physical structure is destroyed, the *energy structure* may remain.

There is extensive controversy regarding this phenomenon because it does not always occur. Does this mean the energy structure doesn't always remain? Or does it mean the sensitive conditions have to be just *perfect* to photograph it? Or does it mean something else entirely? Critics of this effect claim it's caused by incompetent photographers. They say one places the initial sample on a plate, photographs it, then removes it. However, a microscopic residue of moisture is left behind; sort of a water print of the entire leaf. Once the partial leaf is placed back on the same plate, the phantom image is simply a photograph of the old residue. Is this a feasible

2. Could the phantom leaf effect prove that a part of us doesn't die? *Courtesy Robert McGhee*

explanation? Or is it simply a case of the desperate defense lawyer placing the law on trial?

Whatever the case, it's impossible to ponder this phenomenon without thinking of people who lose limbs. In many cases, they describe a haunting sensation afterward.

Joe Bingham is a young man I've known for quite a while. When Joe was a teenager, one of his fingers was cut off in a shop accident. To this day, he describes how he can feel the missing digit. Sometimes it "itches" or "hurts." He almost takes it as an insult when the doctors say it's his imagination. Joe only wishes that were the case. His experience is certainly not unique.

Lots of people who lose limbs experience a "phantom limb." In fact, some amputees think the existence of a phantom limb is crucial in making prosthetics work. It's almost as if the invisible limb merges with the artificial one, creating a more natural connection with the part. On the other hand, people who are born without a limb do not usually experience this phantom sensation. It seems the etheric body may grow and develop along with the physical body. It's only when one part of the equation is suddenly removed—the physical form—that an orphaned energy form is left behind.

Is it possible that the phantom leaf phenomenon and the phantom limb phenomenon are the same? Perhaps the body is composed of more than one layer: a dense physical layer, and an energy layer that seems as intangible as the wind. So far, no one has come forth with a Kirlian photograph of the phantom limb phenomenon. More experimentation is in order.

From a scientific perspective, all matter can more or less be represented by thinking of a complex network of oscillating energies. We perceive energy that oscillates at one frequency and wavelength as visible light. At another, it becomes deadly radiation. At yet another, it heats up your sandwich in the microwave oven. However, all observed reality is basically composed of the same substance—electromagnetic energy—that manifests in many different forms. How might this apply to our bodies?

Ice is water in solid form. If we add energy to ice, it changes form. Heat is a type of energy. When heat is introduced to ice, the molecules begin to speed up and break apart. As they break, and the bonds become loose, the solid becomes a liquid. It's easy to see that the bonds are looser, since we can now pass our hands through the matter. If we add even more energy in the form of heat, the liquid becomes a gas. Obviously, the bonds of steam are even looser than those of liquid. I could add even more energy to create a fourth state of matter: plasma. However, we'll talk about that later.

As you can see, using water as an example, the same substance can appear and behave in an entirely new way simply because it is subjected to a different level of energy. For thousands of years, philosophers and scientists have puzzled over the connection between mind and body. How do we define the mind as different from the brain? The brain is a physical organ, while the mind is the perceived consciousness we experience as our personality, memories, and very existence.

Here is the mind-body dilemma in a nutshell: Based upon empirical evidence, we consider the body physical, while we consider the mind nonphysical. How is it possible for the nonphysical to control the physical? Shouldn't the nonphysical pass right through the physical? How can the two interact?

Perhaps we can answer this question by proposing that the mind and body are not different substances at all, but simply different manifestations of the same substance. The brain is clearly the seat of consciousness. However, our bodies have awareness as well. It's true that our bodies can become paralyzed while our minds still function, but the opposite is also true—our minds can become paralyzed while our bodies still function. They communicate with each other via a detectable pathway of thousands of electromagnetic transmissions per second, traveling two hundred miles per hour.

Is it possible that the etheric body is a layer of you that has just as much physical reality as your fingers and teeth? However, could it exist at a frequency that's not always observable to our naked senses? As we'll discuss later, you see only a tiny fraction of what can be seen. You hear only a tiny fraction of what can be heard. Could we "observe" the mind if we had the proper technology? It's much easier to feel ice than steam, but either way, it's the same thing.

Your consciousness is clearly connected to your body.

Imagine—if it's also connected to this energy layer surrounding our bodies, it may influence us on a regular basis. When simply standing beside someone, humans usually reserve two to three feet of space around their bodies (the amount can vary among different cultures and populations). If someone steps into that space, you can almost feel it. Do we actually feel this person's energy field entering our own? You can experiment with your level of sensitivity by turning your back to a friend and having him or her bring a hand into your field. How often are you able to tell when the hand comes near? You may be startled by your accuracy.

Have you ever met someone whom you did not like for some unexplainable reason? On the other hand, have you ever met someone and everything just clicked, and you immediately felt comfortable? Is it possible that the manner in which our fields react has a direct impact on how we perceive one another? Just as magnets in one position will be attracted while in others they will be repelled, do we have a similar response to other people? We know our bodies are surrounded by fields of energy. It's only logical to realize that those fields interact with the environment.

Is it possible that we may also be able to direct such energies with our eyes? Perhaps that is why eye contact is so meaningful. Have you ever stared at a sleeping person until he or she woke up? This experience is commonly reported. Could it be the product of projecting energy with the eyes? Most people are aware of the imposing sensation when someone stares at the back of your neck. Perhaps we can both send and receive information using this energy field.

Have you ever walked into a room and known a television was on, without hearing or seeing it? If not, try it yourself. Close your eyes and turn on your television. Televisions project significant electromagnetic fields and charges. You might be able to feel this energy in your field. The sensation may be similar to any time in life when one experiences a powerful energy field. Have you walked into a room right after a fight? The environment feels thick and frenzied; hence the phrase "there was so much tension, you could cut it with a knife."

I've also heard of numerous instances where someone in a deep sleep suddenly snapped awake to find a paranormal anomaly in his or her room. The person might see a phantom, or he may notice that each night he awakens at the same time. This could be caused by the body's sensitivity to presences entering the room. If one is awakened at the same time on a regular basis, the patterns should be examined to provide clues as to why a spirit would behave in this way. Is it trying to communicate something? Does the hour have significance?

This receptive energy field around the body is what some call a layer of "psychic energy," though this is certainly a limited usage of the term. As I mentioned in connection to ESP, *psychic* generally refers to using some paranormal sensitivity to gain information. The concept of psychic phenomena has been greatly tainted by big business, 900 phone numbers, and con artists. However, there are some legitimate psychics out there.

If everyone has a field of energy, what exactly is a psychic? What makes them special? Anyone can sit down and pound keys on a piano. However, not everyone can compose and play classical music at age four, like Mozart. Anyone can toss a ball around, but not everyone can score like Michael Jordan. These people are prodigies in their particular skills. People who are *prodigies* in the realm of using etheric energy are considered psychics. The theory holds that almost everyone is capable of using this energy to gain information—in essence, everyone can indeed be psychic. However, some people have the natural ability and/or devoted training to use this sensitivity more efficiently.

AURAS

A lot of psychic phenomena are strongly based upon the presence of an energy field around our bodies. Some claim to see it as an aura of colors surrounding an individual. By interpreting these colors, they draw conclusions about one's general personality and temporary emotions.

Casey Fox, a member of my paranormal research team and near-lifelong friend, has been able to see auras as long as he can remember. Though he can see an individual splashed with his or her own, unique colors, he spent years not knowing what these colors might mean. We've been doing experiments to test his ability and have been impressed so far.

There are some devices on the market known as "aura cameras." They take the biofeedback from a person and interpret it as a colorful aura. It's all a matter of visualizing specific frequencies. At one point, we conducted an experiment in which we compared Fox's vision to what an aura camera captured. We were honestly startled to find that, in most cases, his interpretation, recorded in advance, matched what the camera photographed.

There is also some scientific basis for seeing the aura. We know, without a doubt, that a field of energy surrounds the body. People are not supposed to be able to see such energy, though. However, if a person *could* see this energy, he or she would quite likely see it as colors. Some people are color blind and cannot see what most of us can; on the other hand, is it possible that some people see colors we can't detect?

When we see the color orange, it appears orange because of its low frequency and long wavelength. If we see the color purple, it appears purple because of its high frequency and short wavelength. Ultimately, our eyes differentiate between different kinds of energy by interpreting them as different colors.

Let's say an angry person produces energy that's low frequency with long wavelengths. This is the type of energy that creates the color red. If you are capable of seeing the body's aura in color, and you see the color red, you can assume this person is angry. The same goes for all other colors and the energies—or moods—they represent.

This idea may seem foreign to most people. However, the concept of associating colors with moods is a natural part of our communication. This interpretation has worked its way into our common language. If someone is depressed, he's "blue." A coward is "yellow," and someone might be "green with envy."

Based upon conversations with those who see the aura, as well as authoritative texts, here are some of the most common interpretations of colors in the aura. You will see that they often make traditional sense.

RED—This color represents fiery and dominant qualities. A person with a great deal of drive and force might exude this shade. This color has often been associated with anger, war, and agitation. Remember, it's the competitive color that provokes a bull to charge. This individual wants to succeed.

ORANGE—This is the color of a warm fire. Likewise, it represents warmth and emotion. A person who exudes this color has the ability to connect with others on a friendly, meaningful, and substantial level. This person can open up his or her feelings.

YELLOW—A sunny personality! This person is upbeat, optimistic, and energetic. However, it can also indicate a naïve individual with a superficial perspective. All in all, the color is cheerful.

GREEN—This is the color of vegetation. One can imagine that if a major bomb destroyed a city today, a thousand years from now the ruins would be covered with plants. They are a persistent life-form, and likewise, this color represents perseverance and tenacity. This person is patient and responsible. These are important qualities for success.

BLUE—This is the color of the oceans. And, just as they are unimaginably deep, it indicates depth. Someone with this color has depth in emotion, intuition, and sensitivity. This individual applies significant meaning to life and can affect those around him or her with strong influence. This person is also an aesthetically sensitive lover of beauty.

INDIGO, VIOLET, or PURPLE—These shades have long been associated with magic and mysticism. Who hasn't seen a wizard's purple robe, adorned with glimmering stars and moons? Therefore, this color indicates a mystical or psychic quality. Those who exude this shade are often magnetic or charismatic people who have a unique vision of the world.

BROWN—This is the color of earth. It represents a personality that is grounded and generally sensible. This individual has his or her feet planted firmly on the soil and is wary of a head in the clouds. The downfall to this color is that it can indicate a person who is too dry, cynical, or unimaginative.

WHITE—This color has long been associated with purity, heaven, and infinity. In the same tradition, it is considered an indication of a spiritual person. This is an individual who may focus more on divine issues than worldly ones. Those who claim to have healing ability, or who are drawn to a life of spiritual devotion, such as monks and shamans, often display this color. In light, white is a combination of all colors of the spectrum. Therefore, someone who exudes this should be sensitive to all facets of the human personality and experience.

GRAY—In casual conversation, when we mention a "gray area," we're usually talking about a place of transition, where two defined concepts meet and a nebulous realm is formed. In auras, this color also represents a state of transition or transformation. As one enters a significant new phase in life, gray may indicate this new chapter.

BLACK—In the old westerns, who always wore the black hat? It was the bad guy, of course! In the same sense, this color represents something negative or absent. It can mean there's something wrong with the person's health, or it may indicate something unhealthy about this person's attitude, behavior, or fate. All in all, be wary of this color.

GOLD—Gold has always been considered an attractive and dynamic color. It represents those same qualities in people. Someone with this color may have been given a little extra charm and luck in life. Regardless of what other colors appear in the aura, gold gives this person an edge.

Again, you can see how each color represents qualities we've long associated with that color in language. If you say someone is "blue" to indicate depression, everyone around immediately understands. However, if you say you literally see the color blue around a person, they might suddenly become confused. Is it possible we subconsciously pick up on aura colors, even if we can't actually see them?

TELEKINESIS

The possibility of using the human energy field or mind to directly manipulate the physical environment is called "telekinesis" or "psychokinesis." This could be something as simple as rolling a cigarette across a table with your mind or body energy. Or, it could be something as huge as manipulating the weather.

It's extremely difficult to find someone who claims to possess this ability and will agree to demonstrate it. However, there have been some compelling films made, supposedly under laboratory conditions, that show spectacular displays of alleged telekinesis. Many of these come from recently released Cold War experiments in the Soviet Union. One woman in particular, Nina Kulagina, who died in 1990, was especially amazing. Time and time again she demonstrated her gift before hordes of scientists. Kulagina would place objects under glass boxes, then focus on them, sometimes for hours. Her heart rate and temperature would rise, often to dangerous levels, then the objects would begin to move. In one famous clip, she struggles to move a compass needle under glass. Eventually, the needle begins to move. Then, as she exerts more force, the entire compass itself moves.

In principle, it's easy to see why energy fields, like those around our body, would be capable of manipulating matter. We can manipulate small objects, like scraps of paper, with the body's static electrical potential alone, especially under dry conditions. Is it possible that some people's body energies are stronger than the rest, or can be guided by the person?

On the other hand, look at the curious mechanism by which the mind controls the body. We'll discuss this more later. However, the manner by which the mind controls the body can be considered "mind over matter." Is it possible that in some cases, with some people, the mind's influence can extend past the body? In the same fashion as your mind moves your finger, could it possibly move an object sitting in front of your finger?

There are a variety of tests for telekinesis. You can conduct one of the simplest in minutes. Take a die, visualize what number you want to roll, and toss it. Do it six times, then look at your odds. If you find you can make it land on the number you want more than once, then you may be exercising some telekinetic control over the die. This is a good experiment because you don't have to manufacture "original momentum."

If you stare at something sitting still, and try to will it to move, you're attempting to create original momentum. This means your mind is giving the object that initial push to get it moving. However, this push might be the most difficult part of telekinesis. It is at that point when your mind must overcome its conditioning to create this movement that defies traditional reality. Once you see it begin to move, your brain has broken the mold, and it should be much easier to continue the exercise.

I'll never forget when I finally learned to juggle. My friend gave me three small, identical bean bags with which to practice. I read every bit of available literature and was still completely boggled. I would toss the bags into the air, unsure of what to expect, and each time they would come crashing back down in a display of retarded coordination. There was no reason to believe I would ever be able to juggle. However, I kept trying . . . and trying . . . and trying . . . until, one night, something "magical" happened. I threw them into the air. They came back down. I started grabbing and throwing and . . . son of a gun, I was juggling!

To this day, I have no idea how to explain juggling. I just tell people, throw them around long enough and sooner or later it will happen. I am also a pianist, and I've had similar experiences on the keys. You may find a piece that seems impossible to play. However, if you try to play it often enough, sooner or later your fingers will somehow pull it off. It's difficult to explain really, but it may go back to the idea that the body and mind are one and the same.

When we consider telekinesis, you can see how this applies to original momentum. That sacred moment when it finally happens—when you've trained your mind and body enough to influence physical matter—is probably the most difficult one of all. After that, a sort of automatic response takes over; the product of your body's inherent ability to remember what works and how to repeat the process. For some people, it might be kind of like riding a bike or swimming.

Asian martial artists have long discussed the body's energy and telekinetic potential. They call it "chi" or "ki." They believe this energy is inhaled and exhaled with the air, and that it can be focused to manipulate the physical environment. When I was in my early teens, I was browsing in a martial arts supply store. As I skimmed some books about chi, a woman in a robe approached me and inquired about my interest. We began discussing chi, and she said her instructor was a master of chi manipulation, and she herself had become quite proficient in controlling this energy. The woman asked me to hold out my hand. I complied, and she held her hand over mine. Suddenly, I felt a strong and undeniable wave of "thick" heat extend from her hand to mine. It was a remarkable experience.

Since then, I've heard numerous stories about masters who could easily project this energy with enough force to knock over a paper lantern from twenty feet away. I've also seen footage, shot with a thermal camera, that shows powerful waves of heat extending from the hands of accomplished chi practitioners.

We already know the body has electromagnetic potential. This type of energy alone can significantly influence the environment. We mustn't forget that strong electromagnets are used to toss cars around junkyards. In fact, there are reports and footage of individuals who claim their bioenergy is powerful enough to stick stacks of metal plates on their chests or foreheads. However, I've never seen any watertight laboratory testing of this ability. Are chi practitioners similarly enhancing their natural electromagnetic/electrostatic energy, or tapping something even more powerful? You've probably heard of the "death touch." This is supposedly an example of a martial artist focusing his energy so much that one skillful blow can kill a person.

If you want to develop your telekinetic ability, there is a simple device you can create and use. From a piece of lightweight paper, cut a perfect square roughly three to four inches on each side. Then fold this square diagonally and unfold it. Again, fold it diagonally between the two other corners. You will end up with a pyramid shape.

Next, take a long needle and mount it upright in a base of putty, or by sticking it through a large eraser. Delicately balance your paper pyramid on the needle's point. Of course, the inner apex of the pyramid should rest on the needle's tip. This way, the paper can easily spin with a minimal amount of friction.

Go to a room that is free of air currents and set the apparatus on a table in front of you. Place your hands around the device and imagine the paper pyramid turning in a clockwise or counterclockwise direction (Illus. 3). For the first few minutes, absolutely nothing may occur. Then, out of the blue, the paper may lurch in one direction or another. Once it starts to spin, it may be difficult, if not impossible, to control it. At some points, it may spontaneously stop and start to turn in the opposite direction. Even though it might not be obeying your commands, continue to project commands to it. Eventually, after days, weeks, or months of practice, you may be able to control its behavior at will. Some find it more effective to force energy out, while others prefer to relax and let their natural flow of energy affect the device in a submissive way.

Note that if you blow on the paper, or hold a flame beneath it, usually it will not turn gently but instead will rock violently and come off the needle. If you're especially concerned by air drafts, though, you may want to place it beneath

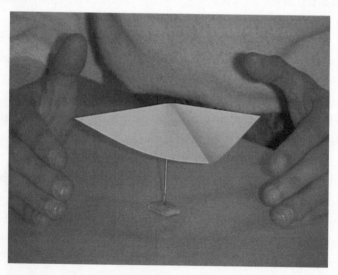

3. A simple device for telekinesis experimentation. *Photo courtesy Joshua P. Warren*

a glass or plastic jar. Many of those who practice with this device on a regular basis claim you can eventually move the paper by simply looking at it. I've also heard of masters who line up twenty of these pinwheels beneath jars and stare at them. Suddenly, one will begin to spin, then another, and another. They react in a sort of scattered shotgun-blast fashion. By refining your ability over time, though, it should become easier and easier to tap your telekinetic potential.

If you do become proficient in generating a telekinetic effect, it's important to demonstrate this for the world. If scientists take a serious interest in it, there's no telling how we could develop thrilling new technologies based upon such a spectacular phenomenon. I once met a woman who claimed to have powerful telekinetic abilities. However, when I asked her to demonstrate her gift, she refused, saying she wouldn't do "parlor tricks." That was ridiculous. What she called parlor tricks I called evidence. She never demonstrated her supposed ability, and her claim only made her look foolish.

The ability to directly influence your physical environment through thought and body energies alone is a fantastic dream of mankind. Movies like *Mary Poppins* and *Star Wars* reinforce this dream. Even though it might be impossible to make a broom sweep your floor, or make a can of beer float out of the fridge and into your hand, you should note that you are not completely isolated from your surroundings, but are indeed a part of them. The level of influence we can attain is still a mystery.

Is it possible that your telekinetic ability is stifled by its enclosure in a physical body? If the body were no longer in the way, would it be easier to affect your environment with thoughts alone? Might this apply to how a ghost can influence the physical world?

We've been pondering some of the more metaphysic

points of the relationship between mind, body, and the physical environment. It might be easy for the most cynical reader to completely dismiss it all as hogwash. However, when it comes to such matters, I hope you'll at least remember this: So many people literally think of their thoughts as "nothing"—private phantoms of fancy that, in and of themselves, do not truly exist. They are considered fleeting entities that cannot be measured or defined by physical standards. This is, in fact, the traditional way of thinking about thoughts. However, I hope you'll remember that, if you look around yourself right now, everything you see—a window, an ink pen, a table, a cup—was first a thought or vision in someone's head before it became a physical reality. Truly, there is an intimate and undeniable relationship between the internal world of the mind and the external world of the body.

TELEPATHY

Communicating by transferring thoughts alone is called "telepathy"—direct mind-to-mind communication. In some cases, it might be the product of mentally broadcasting information electromagnetically. I frequently hear stories about the apparent telepathic link mothers have to their children. Often, when a child is in danger, an intuitive mother comes to the rescue. In fact, I may owe my own life to a similar phenomenon.

When I was around one and a half years old, I was in the backseat of my parents' small station wagon. My mother and father had been driving around town running errands. At one point, I grew sleepy, so I quietly slipped over the backseat, into the farthest section of the car. Soon, I was in peaceful slumber. I had been there for quite some time when, suddenly, my mother was struck with a terrible vision of my

death. She intuitively sensed the vehicle being hit in the rear by another car. In a strange sort of panic, my mother climbed over the seats, took me into her arms, and placed me back in my car seat. In a matter of seconds, the vehicle was indeed violently rear-ended. My head had been an inch from the tail-gate, and that area was completely crushed. If she hadn't moved me when she did, I would certainly have been killed. Though an incident like this could obviously be viewed as some session of seeing the future—a premonition, if you will—it also may have involved some psychic connection between mother and baby, some type of telepathic relation-ship. After so many years of evolution, is it possible that a paranormal mechanism to protect one's child has developed?

The most widely practiced form of telepathy is prayer. Prayer is usually considered a session in which the subject's mind directly communicates with the mind of God or some other divine element. Oftentimes, people who pray say they don't believe in "psychic activity," though prayer clearly falls into the category of telepathy. This is another good example of how religion and science may view the same phenomenon in different ways.

Television and radio towers broadcast information to your house twenty-four hours a day. They send these signals as electromagnetic waves. Look at the amount of information waves can carry. You can watch your favorite television show in dazzling colors and with stereo surround sound. For all practical purposes, the information arrives instantly; and when using a satellite, you can even interact via phone lines! The electromagnetic waves that accomplish all this are no dif-ferent from the ones around your body; they vary only by frequency and wavelength. Is it possible we might have the potential to be human broadcasting towers? The same antenna is capable of both sending and receiving. Might we sometimes send and receive thoughts, but we're not all on the same channel? In experiments, some people seem to be better receivers, and others better senders. It's easy to experiment yourself.

You and a friend can easily test your telepathic compatibility with a simple method. Think of a number between one and five, stare at your friend, and see if he or she can guess it. When some people receive messages, they claim to actually see the number; others only sense it in some intuitive way. I often hear of people who close their eyes and visualize a white screen. Sooner or later, the answer simply appears on the screen. If you have a high rate of success with a friend, find out who's best at sending or receiving. Then repeat the experiment, recording results, gradually expanding to a larger range of numbers. I've seen telepathic couples guess a series of numbers between one and a thousand with startling accuracy.

We're so familiar with how radio waves are broadcast that it's simple to compare telepathy to such electromagnetic transmissions. However, there are some possible faults with using this analogy. For one thing, the literature is filled with stories about telepathic communications between two people on different parts of the globe. This is especially the case between husbands and wives when one is off at war and some trauma is experienced. If such tales are true, it's difficult to explain how the body could project fields at such a distance. Also, experiments have been done between telepathic couples when one was placed inside a Faraday Cage, a box that seals out electric fields. The cage didn't seem to affect accuracy. However, you must never forget that X rays have always been around, but they weren't discovered until 1895. Does the mind operate at a frequency and scale far too advanced to be blocked by any substance—and, in fact, *that's* why our technology is too crude to even measure it? At some point, will we learn to detect and harness it just like microwaves? On the other hand, as with telekinesis, is it also capable of doing the opposite: not passing through objects, but resisting them in order to move them? Perhaps the energy of the mind can work at levels both too high and too low for us to currently understand.

COLLECTIVE ESP AND SYNCHRONICITY

In trying to understand psychic activity, there is one peculiar phenomenon that warrants at least a mention. When studying the paranormal, it is important to be aware of all known possibilities. The psychic abilities mentioned thus far have generally focused on individuals. However, ESP may manifest collectively within a group of people. This opens some unique and complex topics.

Life is an infinite chain reaction of causes and effects. Each individual affects every other individual—or, no man is an island, as they say. For example, maybe you can say you wouldn't be reading this book right now if you hadn't seen it on the shelf. Then, maybe you'd never have seen it on the shelf if you hadn't decided to stop by the bookstore on the way home. Then, maybe you wouldn't have been in that bookstore if you'd taken the job in the next town instead. And so on. You can trace your life back to a series of connected events that reaches your birth, and even before . . . clear to the beginning of the beginning. It's only natural that life's events take on some sort of geometric design—a natural pattern, mathematically precise—that is usually too intricate and complex to follow.

Every moment, an infinite series of chain reactions is taking place all around, and even inside, you. You'll never know how many times you might have been killed by a reckless driver if you'd left a restaurant ten seconds later, or ten seconds earlier. You'll never know if you'd have lived one minute more if you'd not eaten that second helping of bacon. However, sometimes the design of your life comes together right in front of you.

A few months ago, someone brought up an old friend's name. He'd moved to a distant town and I hadn't heard from the guy in nearly three years. Within thirty seconds the phone rang. Yep. It was him! I can't even remember the last time I'd spoken of the guy. What happened there?

Have you ever, out of the blue, thought about an old, obscure movie and how you miss it? Then, did you flip through the channels to find it airing that night? What happened there?

How many times have you been trying to avoid a specific person, and lo and behold, he or she shows up in the strangest location? You could say the phone call incident was telepathic: I thought of my friend and he called me, or, he intended to call me, and that caused my other friend to tell me. You could say the movie thing is telekinetic: that your desire to see the movie caused it to play that night. You could even say you'd seen the future. But these things seem a little different from traditional psychic phenomena. That's because they're more situational. It just happened that things worked out in a way that appeared to be more than blind coincidence. Is this the product of people being subconsciously psychic? Or are these simply places where the mathematical connections in your life join right in front of you? Do you notice something only 1 percent of the time it happens, then assume it's a rare and exciting occurrence?

When you find strange and remarkable "coincidences" happening all around you, it's called "synchronicity." It's based on the idea that everything is working smoothly and you're in step with what you're supposed to be doing, or maybe *not* supposed to be doing. Either way, humans can interpret these moments in life to apply a sense of meaning to how and why these occurrences take place.

As you experiment with various types of psychic phenomena, always be cognizant of synchronicity. When something amazing happens, is it because someone consciously initiated it, or because things just "magically" fell into place? This is one way of saying that certain things in life happen for a reason. When you observe an extraordinary phenomenon, is it *really* extraordinary? Or are you just witnessing an extraordinary moment initiated by life? Either way, we are each truly connected to everyone and everything.

Humans are joined in many ways. When I stand four feet in front of you, it might seem as though there's nothing between us. But, there is. It's air. A wall of air connects the tip of my nose to the tip of yours. However, unrestricted air molecules are loose enough that you can push your hand right through. If you wave your hand hard enough, the air will move and a breeze will lift my bangs. Most don't visualize air this way, though, because they can't see it or usually feel it. You can see that we're joined in a direct, physical way in this manner. Also, as we've discussed, our body energies interact. Even our very thoughts are connected. Did you invent the word *soft?* Nope. Someone taught it to you, just like someone taught it to me. But when we both hear the word *soft,* we know what that means. We're intellectually connected.

As you explore the hidden world—the world of the unknown—keep a watchful eye out for connections. Whatever you make of reality, it's certainly a complex network. Some parts are visible, while others are invisible. Be aware of how "normal" reality functions: Precisely how do psychic phenomena fit in?

DEATH

The human body is more than what meets the eye. Just as we have a unique physical body, we have a unique energy body. As you've seen, there's no doubt that this energy body exists. In this modern age of technology, we've documented its presence, but people have discussed this field for thousands of years in reference to psychic abilities. Is it indeed possible that our energy fields hold the key to understanding ESP?

Regardless of how these energies behave in life, they may have a great influence on us after death. If your body consists of a physical layer—like ice—and a ghostly layer—like steam—is it possible that one layer could die, while the other still carries on? The Law of Conservation of Energy states that energy can be neither created nor destroyed, simply conserved. Does that mean the energy disperses back into nature and our consciousness ends? Or when our physical bodies die, might this energy structure continue to exist? As the old saying goes, we may literally "give up the ghost," discarding our shell of flesh. If a physically destroyed limb leaves some aspect behind, why shouldn't an entire body? If our flesh is indeed only one layer of a multilayered being, then we may shed it and still exist in some alternative form. If the phantom leaf phenomenon is legitimate, it could prove that a part of us does not die. But, is this part of us still conscious?

Some people do not believe in the existence of the mind. Those people generally think living creatures are no more than organic computers. They propose that we are highly complex biological machines, but solely mechanical creatures nonetheless. If such were the case, we would merely shut down at death. In this way, the human experience is limited to the time between birth and death. On a cosmic scale, individual life would therefore be worthless—having no eternal meaning. Is a belief in the afterlife merely a hopeful way of giving our lives nonexistent meaning? Should we thereby resort to hedonism, free from spiritual consequence and responsibility?

The great philosopher René Descartes pondered this complex issue more than three hundred years ago. He wanted to know the ultimate truth in life. Therefore, he conducted a mental experiment: Descartes doubted everything about the world he could possibly doubt, believing that what remained must be truth. He found there was only one thing he could not deny—that he was doubting, that he was *thinking*. He then uttered the immortal statement, "I think, therefore I am."

Let me clarify the significance. Our five physical senses trick us every day. Objects far away appear to shrink, while those coming closer appear to grow. The top of a nearby trash can may be a circle, but when we place it at an angle ten feet away, it becomes an oval. Humans jump to ridiculous conclusions based upon their inaccurate perceptions. Professional magicians, or illusionists, exploit this weakness. The weakness can be further demonstrated when we acknowledge that not everyone sees the world the same way. Again, color blindness is a prime example. Or, remember the chocolate example: I like the taste of chocolate. You may like the taste of chocolate as well. But how do you know we taste the same thing? It's a taste we both enjoy, and one we can distinguish from other tastes. But you don't know if we experience the same taste. And in this life, you never will.

There is enormous inconsistency in how we view the physical world. But there is one thing we all have in common. Everything we can see, hear, smell, taste, or touch is destined for decay. Anything we can physically perceive, including the human body, has a limited life span—whether seconds or aeons. And while everything around us is fleeting and temporary, the only thing we know for certain is that we possess an ability that a chair does not: to think. Our bodies lock us, like prisoners, into this physical realm. But a mental entity—a mental experience—what we shall call the mind—does exist. It is a mystery in life and it is a mystery in death. "I think, therefore I am" . . . not "I have a body, therefore I am."

There is also surprisingly simple scientific evidence for the existence of the mind. In his book *Windows on the Mind*, Erich Harth illustrates this:

> *If I want to sit down and write a letter, this "want" must cause the brain to send signals to the appropriate muscles. To a physicist, this is a disconcerting thought because it would mean that a nonphysical entity, the mind, is able to exert a physical influence on the body.*

How can something that does not exist cause a physical reaction, like moving your body at will? How could there be a physical effect without a physical cause? This goes back to the mind-body dilemma. There seems to be only one explanation for how this thing called the mind could manipulate a two-hundred-pound chunk of flesh like me. It *does* exist. Whatever it is, it's *there*.

Now there will be some of you reading this text who might think: Hmmm . . . but what if a *chair* is conscious? And how about plants? Can they think?

Remember all the talk about gray areas in science—places where there are gaps in the collective understanding? Drawing the line between plants and animals seems to be one of them. What's a sponge? They say it's an animal, but it just sits there. Look at an ameba. It has no brain, no eyeballs, no sense of humor; it's only a single cell! Yet even an ameba hunts down food and eats it. Is it conscious? Does a paramecium have memories? Look at a Venus's-flytrap. It's a plant with juicy jaws and long teeth, and its mouth snaps shut fast, yet an adult sponge (an animal) never moves! Is a tree conscious? It moves: the motion is slow, but it moves. Keep in mind, you and I move slowly compared to a common roach (their brains process motion faster than ours). Trees also carry out intelligent food-making processes and reproduce. Some people claim plants will respond and grow healthier when exposed to classical music.

Can anyone say for sure whether plants are conscious? No, of course not. But they are organic, living entities. When it comes to something inanimate—a rock, for example— there's no reason to believe it has any consciousness. In fact, if we insinuate that it does, it might be an insult to organic creatures. Some religions believe all things possess a soul. Though certainly a fascinating concept, it's lacking in evidence.

We know that humans have an energy layer and we can accept the existence of a mind. We know, according to the Law of Conservation of Energy, that energy can be neither created nor destroyed, but simply conserved or transferred into another form. When your physical body dies, it is possible that another aspect of yourself—one of pure energy and thought— still exists. Is this what we might sometimes call a ghost?

WHY DOES AN ENTITY STICK AROUND?

Try to view entities as humans in another form. They are a mind and energy that still retains specific, individual identity. We cannot scientifically know if there is an ultimate destination for any spirit—*that* question is pondered by religion. But there are certain variables that clearly heighten the chance that a ghost will stay on the physical plane.

If a person dies young, especially violently, it is likely that a ghost will remain. This falls into the "unfinished business" category. A young person's natural tendency is to live out a full biological life span. When that opportunity is suddenly stripped away, it seems a stubbornness frequently kicks in. Based on my research, most parents who bury a child encounter that child's spirit at some point. Traditional psychologists claim this experience is a common hallucination, a way for the grieving, traumatized parents to fill the sense of loss and comfort themselves. Then again, it seems any experience that scientists can't explain is eventually called a hallucination. Oftentimes, a young person's spirit will stay for a period of a few years, then eventually move on. If the child is extremely young, it may stay due simply to confusion.

I once interviewed a family who grew up primarily on a secluded Alabama farm. The house had been passed down for at least two generations. There was no hospital nearby, and in the early 1900s, a baby was born in the attic. The birth was difficult. It was the mother's sixth pregnancy. While giving birth, she almost died, barely pulling through. However, the sickly infant died after only a few days. From then on, for generations, the baby's spirit haunted the farmhouse.

The activity began the very night after the baby died. The other little children, three brothers and two sisters, huddled together in the middle of the bedroom, quivering in fear as the baby's tormented screams wailed from the dark, empty attic. They would hold their ears and cry, terrified by the ghost baby's relentless agony. At other times, small objects would fall off low shelves. They eventually sold the old house and left the decades-old activity behind. You can imagine the confusion this infant soul must have felt.

Of course, unfinished business is most common among older people. Usually, when an older person chooses to stay after death, it's because of a strong connection to the physical world. This is especially so with extremely rich people who obviously don't want to leave their fortunes behind. One slaves away to build up money in this lifetime, and I'm sure it can be difficult to leave the fruits of that hard work behind! In many other cases, it seems riches are not necessary, as long as the person loved the location. Some people simply do not want to leave their home behind. It's a place in which they grew to feel comfortable. In some cases, owning the property was the person's life achievement.

I conducted an in-depth investigation of a farmstead in the mountains of western North Carolina. An old man and woman worked their entire lives to attain their dream home. It was a grand farmhouse, built of rich chestnut, next to a crystal-clear lake. A mountain peak towered beside it, its reflection spilling across the shiny water. To this day, the location is surreal. It's easy to see why they fell in love with the place.

After the man became old, he finally grew tired of working the farm. He was especially fed up with snowy winters and decided he wanted to spend his last years sunbathing on the Florida coast. He proposed to his wife that they sell the property. She glared in outraged disbelief and told him she would never, ever part with the farm. They fought over the issue until, a couple of months later, a local rich man made a generous offer for the place. The old man went into town and signed over the deed. When he returned to the house, he found his wife hanging from an apple tree. A white owl sat on the limb from which the old woman swung. He looked deep into the owl's bright yellow eyes and, with a chill, knew he was staring into his wife's seething face. The owl flew away.

Within a week, the old man's salt-and-pepper hair turned completely white. He packed up his bags and left town, never to be seen again. It seems he never overcame the shock. The white owl is still seen flapping through the night air or watching silently from the tree line. Does the old woman really appear as the owl? It's difficult to say since it's hard to catch an owl. But, if so, this is a good example of someone so attached to a worldly possession—property—that she refused to leave it behind.

There are other people who stick around because they don't want to leave *someone* behind. These can be the creepiest spirits. It seems they like to watch the person they're haunting in a voyeuristic way. Ghosts sometimes haunt their widowed spouses for this reason. Such phantoms can be possessive, and often do more harm than good by continuing to stay on this plane, attached to one person. Perhaps the worst of these are revenge seekers. Murder victims frequently haunt their killers, obsessed with exacting supernatural vengeance.

One haunted mansion I've researched is inhabited by the spirit of a chambermaid. In the 1920s, she was having an affair with her employer, a charismatic doctor. His wife, a cold and hateful woman, knew about the infidelity but tolerated it. However, after the doctor died, the maid and the widowed wife finally had a fight. The chambermaid was pushed down the stairs to her death. Afterward, her spirit returned to incessantly haunt the wife, eventually driving her to madness.

Those with a guilty conscience may choose to stay as well. They fear the consequences of possibly moving on to a realm of judgment. It's certainly an understandable situation. As Isaac Newton said, for every action, there's an opposite but equal reaction. In other words, you reap what you sow. Call it karma if you like. But if you were a cruel person in life, you will obviously have more anxiety about the possibility of having to take responsibility for your behavior. If you could procrastinate by lingering here on earth, would you do so?

It seems some spirits stay around because they truly do not realize they're dead. This type of situation is illustrated well by the 1999 film *The Sixth Sense*. After the World Trade Center fell, I began hearing of paranormal experiences around the location. People who lived near the site would sometimes see apparitions of people in business suits wandering around the community as if in a complete daze. Do these people know they are dead? Or are they still in the ultimate shock? How much longer will their phantoms wander those heavy streets?

Human behavior is complex and mysterious. The behavior of ghosts is the same. Determining why a conscious specter stays around is one of the most challenging questions facing the ghost hunter. In our world of the living, we often can't explain human motivation. Why do some people commit brutal, grue-some crimes? Often they'll simply tell you what horrific serial killer Ed Gein said: "I felt compelled to do it." Understanding the psychology of a ghost is an even more daunting task. For that reason, prospective methods of communication have been sought since the beginning of recorded history. Attempting to communicate with the dead is called "necromancy." Whether using a medium or Ouija board, or things more complex like video cameras and tape recorders, paranormal researchers have desperately tried to establish direct communication with spir-its. Unfortunately, little documentable progress has been made. Later, we'll explore this area more fully.

HOW DOES A GHOST INTERACT WITH THE WORLD?

Ghosts are nonphysical entities. We can define *nonphysical* as "not being restricted to the known laws of physical matter." We've been pondering the possibility that spirits operate on a frequency different from that of dense physical matter, sometimes preventing the two from interacting. But if a ghost is nonphysical, how can it interact with the physical world? This enigma takes us back to the mind-body dilemma. Most are familiar with the classic image of a cartoon ghost trying to hug someone but simply passing right through the person. If ghosts are nonphysical, how can we see them? How can they move objects? How can they touch us? How can we hear them? We enter a highly theoretical realm when addressing such subjects.

A common magnet emanates strong lines of force from its poles. These fields clearly interact with the physical environment, yet we cannot see, feel, hear, taste, or smell them. To our bare human senses, they are truly nonexistent. Magnets do have a strong effect on iron filings, of course. Therefore, if we sprinkle hundreds of iron filings on a piece of paper, then place the magnet below them, the filings adhere to the lines of

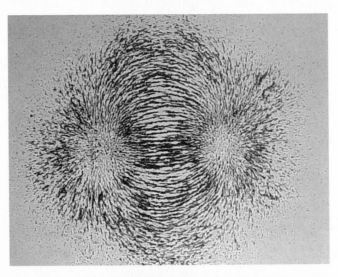

4. Iron filings clearly show a magnet's lines of force. *Photo courtesy Joshua P. Warren*

force. Though we cannot see the actual fields, we can observe a *physical representation* of the fields (Illus. 4). This method gives us a practical means of studying the lines, and yet we still do not see the actual lines themselves.

Lines of force bulge from around the poles of a magnet three-dimensionally. If we surround a magnet with iron filings, its field becomes visible three-dimensionally (Illus. 5). The invisible form quickly emerges, almost like a materialized phantom.

Perhaps the residual, conscious energy left behind by a physically dead human can operate in much the same way. Even though a spirit is nonphysical, just like the magnetic lines of force, it may be able to interact with the physical world, just like the magnetic lines of force. Imagine it like this: Your body is composed of lots of tiny building blocks — cells. Likewise, a magnet's invisible lines of force cannot

5. When a magnet is surrounded by iron filings, its lines of force create a three-dimensional form. *Photo courtesy Joshua P. Warren*

materialize without tiny building blocks. Of course, these building blocks are the iron filings. But if a magnet's fields can be represented by iron filings, what substance might a ghost use? If your visible body is made of cells, what is a spirit's visible body made of? It seems they frequently use free-floating static electrical charges in the air, called "ions."

When someone comes into contact with a spirit, he or she often reports the following phenomena: hair standing on end, cold chills, three-dimensional light forms, objects moving. All of these activities can be duplicated using ions.

Let me clarify exactly what static electricity is. Static electricity (or electrostatic energy) is not the kind that comes from your wall socket or a battery. The electricity that comes from your wall is an alternating current (AC) that switches back and forth between positive and negative at sixty cycles per second (in the United States). What comes from a battery is a steady stream of electricity that does not switch polarity. This is direct current (DC). Static electricity is naturally available in the environment around us. Lightning is created by static electricity. Getting a shock off a doorknob in winter is also the product of static electricity. It's based upon the balance of electrical particles. If you rub your socks on the carpet, charges build up on your body. Those extra charges jump off, or discharge, when they get near the metal conductor. Lightning is caused by charges building up between the clouds and ground, or sometimes cloud to cloud, then balancing with a massive discharge.

There are novel devices that are made to produce hundreds of thousands of volts of static electricity for science demonstrations. Though the voltage, or amount, of electricity is high, the amperage, or power, is low. They can deliver a powerful shock, but they're much safer than using a high-amperage, low-voltage generator. Some of the most popular that educators commonly use in the classroom are Van de Graaff generators and Wimshurst/Bonetti machines (Illus. 6). The Van de Graaff is the most well-known. It is the large, silver spheroid, atop a plastic base, that will make a student's hair stand on end. This is an obvious example of how ions affect hair in this way. As most know from elementary school, two identical charges (+ + or - -) repel each other, while two different charges (+ - or - +) attract each other. When someone comes into contact with strong static electricity, his or her flesh and hair are exposed to the same charges. This makes the hair push away from the flesh, thereby standing up.

Electrical charges rushing across the skin also create an "ion wind." This produces a cool or cold sensation on the flesh. It is the result not just of moving air, but also moving electrical particles. This could certainly account for cold chills when a ghost is encountered.

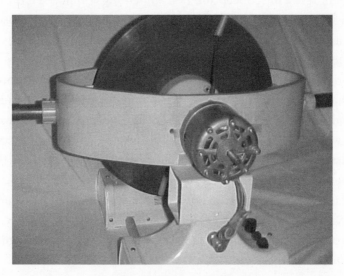

6. A Wimshurst/Bonetti electrostatic generator.
Photo courtesy Joshua P. Warren

Ion wind has another bizarre quality: As this current of energy passes over your flesh, not only is it cold, but it actually feels like you're being touched. Sometimes, in demonstrations, I have a volunteer from the audience turn away from me. I lift an electrostatic generator and blow a quick ion wind across the person's shoulder. The subject always thinks he or she has been touched on the back. I've experienced that sensation several times in haunted houses. The hair on the back of my neck will stand.

When a spirit is seen, we call this an "apparition." It is generally a three-dimensional form that may look entirely structured, like a human, or more abstract, like a mist or a globe of light. Spirits sometimes appear translucent but are often reported as being opaque, just like physical matter. How can this be? We must keep in mind that, when we look at a car, for example, all we are really seeing is the light reflected from the matter. The car, nonetheless, still appears solid. It is a misconception that something composed entirely of light must be translucent. *Everything* we see is composed entirely of light, or the lack thereof. Conceptually, seeing a ghost is no different from seeing a living person.

Using concentrated ions, we can create three-dimensional images. Such forms become visible as *plasma.* Solid, liquid, and gas are the first three known states of matter. However, few people are familiar with the fourth state of matter—plasma. This is especially peculiar since 99 percent of the known universe exists in the plasma state. In order to explain plasma, I'll use water as an example again. Water molecules are made of atoms. Each atom contains a balanced number of protons (positive charges) and electrons (negative charges). Therefore, the atom has a neutral charge, since each type of charge cancels out the other. If we add heat energy to solid water, the molecules spread apart and we get liquid. If we add even more energy, they spread apart farther to produce a gas. But if we add even *more* energy, one or more electrons are ripped right out of the atoms. That leaves a mixture of free-floating electrons and atoms that now have a positive charge (since their electron balance is gone), making them positive ions. So, a typical plasma is a mixture of electrons and positive ions. The product is usually a brilliant, glowing display of electrical energy.

A common form of plasma is an ordinary candle flame. Think about it: It's not a solid, it's not a liquid, nor a gas. When all else fails, you've got a plasma. Neon bulbs produce plasma inside, and almost everyone has seen "plasma balls." They're the glass globes filled with snapping fingers of blue or pink electricity. You generally find them used for eclectic decoration, especially around Halloween. Lightning bolts, however small or large, are a form of plasma.

I should clarify that plasma and ectoplasm are not synonymous. *Plasma* is a physics term, while *ectoplasm* usually refers to an unscrupulous tool used by fake nineteenth-century mediums. During the Victorian era, belief in contacting the dead, called "spiritualism," became big business. Mediums were in heated competition with one another. Obviously, the more bizarre and extreme a séance was, the more it was discussed. Word of mouth generated by a shocking experience translated directly into dollar signs. Because of this, a slew of innovative tricks were developed and used to manipulate the specter-hungry audiences.

At séances, mediums would sometimes secrete a thick, gooey, usually white substance, from body orifices. It might drip from the nostrils, ooze from the ears, work its way up from the throat, or exude from areas even more embarrassing. The mediums called it ectoplasm and claimed it was a mysterious by-product of spiritual interaction in the physical world. The idea of ectoplasm seems absurd to most serious paranormal researchers. It was apparently invented and used solely for its grotesque and dramatic impact on observers.

The term was also popularized by the 1984 release of the film *Ghostbusters*. On the big screen, it looks great to see a hideous goblin drench an investigator with bright, colorful mucus. Fortunately, real ghost hunters don't get slimed. If they did, I'm pretty sure I'd be in a different field.

Some researchers *do* simply refer to ectoplasm as *whatever* substance ghosts utilize for materialization. In that sense, they can use the words *plasma* and *ectoplasm* interchangeably. I would not recommend this, however, as the word *ectoplasm* has become tainted by its sordid history and popular usage in silly movies. Besides, based upon our current evidence and theories, it seems ghosts often materialize in a state of *plasma*.

Just like a ghost, raw electricity is invisible. But when it becomes visible, you are actually seeing it as a plasma. An electrical spark between two electrodes is a plasma—that means the air, or gas, between the electrodes changed states of matter while the voltage passed through. Plasmas are conductive and allow high-enough voltages to pass through the air more easily. However, there are different kinds of plasmas. Though usually blue or white, electricity can appear in a variety of colors, tints, and tones. A well-known example of an electrical light form is Saint Elmo's fire. During the Age of Exploration, when the oceans were filled with superstitious seamen, it was not uncommon for a ship to be caught in a rising storm. Sometimes, as the storm built, sailors would gaze at the topmasts to find them surrounded by an eerie blue glow. They took this as an auspicious sign from Saint Elmo, assuring them of his protection. Actually, this effect was caused by a buildup of electrical particles. As the storm clouds swirled and rushed around the ship, the topmasts would build up charges. Eventually, the charges would grow too great to occupy the surface of the masts, and they would disperse into the atmosphere. The dispersing particles glowed, creating the "corona effect." If you'll remember, this is the same effect photographed by Kirlian techniques. In fact, you could consider a Kirlian photo an example of induced Saint Elmo's fire.

An object that's round can store a great deal of electrical charges on its surface. That's why lots of static-electrical generators build the energy on a large metal ball. However, charges leak off sharp points. It is around such points where a corona of electrical light is usually most pronounced. Cowboys enjoyed sharing spooky stories about the effect. Sometimes, at dusk, when a storm was blowing in, wranglers were shocked upon looking over their herd of cattle. Blue flames would spray from the steers' horns. It was a truly devilish scene, and it inspired legends of phantom herds.

Today, Saint Elmo's fire is most frequently observed on the propellers and wing tips of airplanes. As the metal craft cuts through the atmosphere, enormous charges can be produced that stream away as the mysterious blue glow. Modern ships still experience the effect from time to time as well. The discharge can create plasma light forms of almost any design.

Using electrical charges, it is also possible to move objects. This can be simply demonstrated by rubbing a plastic comb briskly through your hair. Afterward, it may be possible to move small objects, like threads, Ping-Pong balls, cigarettes, scraps of paper, etc., by bringing them near the comb. You can even manipulate water. If you turn on your faucet to produce a thin stream of water and place the comb nearby, the stream will bend toward the comb. Once it touches the plastic, the comb will discharge and the water will drop back. Of course, these are only small-scale examples of electrostatic potential. The stronger the charge, the larger the items that can be moved.

Residents of haunted houses frequently report finding one area of a room in shambles. A previously neat stack of papers might be strewn everywhere, or a line of pictures on a wall will be crooked. It seems almost as if a burst of passing energy had affected the items in an extreme and uncontrolled way.

The exact relationship between electrostatic charges and electromagnetism (the two most prevalent manifestations of ghostly energy) is still a mysterious realm of science. In fact, it seems many of our great future discoveries depend on our understanding of it. However, we know the power of an electromagnet. You can quickly build one to experiment. Simply take an iron nail and wrap a piece of thin, insulated wire around it a few dozen times, creating a coil. Then attach each end of the wire to a big 6-volt flashlight battery. When hooked to the battery, you'll find you have created a significant electromagnet. It's easy to manipulate small metal objects with it. Unlike a piece of natural magnetite, this device produces a field that can be delicately adjusted—made stronger or weaker by changing the number of coils or the electrical power passed through the wire.

It should be clear that focused electricity is certainly capable of producing strong physical forces. Electrical charges literally bind the universe. At our smallest levels, you and I are nothing more than charges. A ghost could theoretically be as strong as, or even stronger than, a person.

Using an electrostatic generator in the laboratory, I have caused a subject's hair to stand on end, given him or her chills, made him perceive a physical touch, manipulated objects from a distance, and created three-dimensional plasma light forms. Since all these elements, and more, can be created by focusing charges, a relationship between electricity and ghostly phenomena becomes apparent. But what *exactly* might this relationship be?

I have found, in my personal research, that most significant ghostly encounters seem to take place during the cold, dry months (late September through early March in North America). These are also the times of year when static electricity is usually most active. During the fall and winter, it's not uncommon to receive a surprise shock from a doorknob. Whenever the conditions are right for producing static electricity, it seems they are also most conducive to ghostly activity. This appears to reaffirm a spirit's dependency on electrical charges and, thereby, the environment as well.

I was a guest on a national radio show several years ago and began discussing the connection between static electricity and ghostly phenomena. We received a call from a gentleman who used to work in a haunted neon-light factory. He recalled going into the dark shop by himself one evening. The sky was restless, and he described a natural feeling of static-electrical energy in the air. Upon entering the shop, the hair on his arms and neck suddenly stood on end. He was shocked to find a luminous apparition staring from across the room. It was a woman in loose garb, her features nebulous yet glowing. Needless to say, he was stunned. As the apparition lingered, neon bulbs around her brightened. This is what happens to a neon tube when subjected to a stream of charges. After only a few seconds, the specter disappeared. The neon bulbs blinked out, but the air was still thick with electricity.

When the air is especially humid, it's filled with more moisture. Obviously, water conducts electricity. Therefore, electrical charges leak away into the air's water. Because of this, it's much more difficult to build up large charges. Almost as soon as they collect, they disperse into the atmosphere. However, when it is dry, the air is more of an *insulator*, a substance that doesn't conduct electricity. In dry weather, larger charges are more easily created, and the impact of a static-electrical phenomenon is maximized. This principle changes a bit during electrical storms. Despite the moisture, the air contains an enormous amount of ions. Under such conditions, you might find enhanced activity as well. It gives some credence to the classic introduction: "It was a dark and stormy night . . ."

It seems that, in order to interact with the physical world, a ghost may sometimes use electrical charges to create a temporary physical form. Remember the magnet's lines of force? We can't see them, but we can see a physical representation of them using tiny particles: iron filings. Does a ghost also create a physical representation of itself using tiny particles: electrical charges? Under ideal conditions, a ghost might sometimes manipulate electrical fields and charges to gain access to our world.

In the classic 1933 movie *The Invisible Man,* with Claude Raines, it was obviously impossible to see him. Therefore, he wrapped himself in bandages. This created a physical representation of his body. Perhaps, for ghosts to physically interact, they must wrap themselves in a "bandage" of ions. Controlling these charges could allow ghosts to be seen and to move objects. In fact, spirits could accomplish most of the spectacular activity attributed to them in this way. If we are correct to assume that an entity's manifestation may have some dependence on the electrical environment, we can use this knowledge to gain advantages in predicting and manipulating them.

If you are to hunt ghosts, you can increase your chances of success by going to an environment most conducive to the activity. It's no different from a fisherman's heading to the sea. Though it seems almost any location can lend itself to phantasmal occurrences, some areas are obviously more active than others. Cold, dry environments are always a good bet.

If spirits do indeed use charges as building blocks to manifest, then perhaps a ghost hunter can heighten the chances of a ghostly encounter by enhancing the electrical environment. This can be done by using a Van de Graaff, Wimshurst/Bonetti, or similar static-electricity generator to pump ions into the atmosphere. It may add to the environment those extra building blocks necessary for a ghost to *materialize,* or create an interactive, physical body. By the same token, one might be able to prevent ghostly interaction with the physical world by preventing the buildup of charges in an area. Both of these possibilities will be explored later.

So far, you've seen how a human's conscious energy body might be able to remain after the death of the physical body. Now, based upon examining electrical principles, you can understand how this nonphysical body might be able to participate in the physical world on a limited basis. In our physical lives, some people are stronger or more capable than others. If entities must use atmospheric energy to materialize, then surely some beings are better at that skill than others. In a general sense, maybe a "haunted area" is a place where resident entities have the power, or perhaps more importantly, the will, to intrude upon our realm. It might be the product of a unique combination: an entity, that entity's power and intention, and environmental factors. These environmental factors could include the electromagnetic and electrostatic atmosphere, geomagnetic influences, or any number of variable conditions, perhaps still unknown to science. This model of ghostly activity implies that some might be caused by a parallel realm that coexists with our own. It's one of invisible life that becomes detectable to us on a rare basis. Though this is a neat and traditional package of theory that can be applied to most entity phenomena, as always, it falls short of accurately explaining all reality. The activity of proposed entities becomes a sloppy matter, a mishmash of all kinds of diverse manifestations. New questions arise.

Why do some spirits appear human, while others look more abstract? It's not uncommon to hear of someone seeing a full-bodied apparition. Lots of times, the individual doesn't realize that he or she is staring at a ghost until the figure vanishes. Sometimes, ghosts are most definitely believed to be people. Over the past year, I've been investigating the home of a young woman who had repeated encounters with an apparition so well materialized that she believed it was a living intruder. The first time she saw this phantom in her home, she called 911 to report a break-in. It was difficult for her to finally accept that the "man in her home" was actually a ghost.

On the other hand, it's even more common for people to see a phantom that does not so clearly resemble a typical human. Mists are often seen. Strangely enough, these mists don't always appear the way you would imagine. In 2001, I encountered a mist face-to-face. A fellow researcher and I were in the attic of an extremely haunted residence. As I was exiting the attic, the other researcher shouted, "Look!" Between us, a blue-gray mist swirled in the air. It was contained within a patch of air two or three feet in diameter. It didn't behave like a puff of smoke. Instead, it lingered without dispersing, moving in waves that seemed angular and traditionally geometric in design. After ten to fifteen seconds, it dimmed and vanished.

In addition, some encounter spirits as balls of light. Lots of ghost photographs show circles, spheres, and ellipses generally called "orbs"(Illus. 7). These appear especially when photographing, videotaping, or otherwise monitoring the infrared realm. Video cameras that can shoot into the deeper infrared spectrums frequently show orbs zipping around haunted locations. So far, it seems the best shutter speed is about thirty frames per second—the same as traditional video. What are these paranormal orbs? Are they spirits? We can't say for sure. But they do seem to be most prevalent at haunted locations. Therefore, there is certainly some connection. Sometimes, one huge orb is seen lumbering along. At other times, a flurry sweeps by. Is it possible that one part of a spirit—his or her very heart, if you will—occupies the infrared, but the body occupies another realm? Could we be taping one aspect of the soul, so to speak?

On the other hand, there are those who say all orbs are nothing but reflections, dust, insects, or some other common particle. Indeed, it's easy to capture an orblike image by photographing a particle or catching a tricky reflection. Drops of moisture, like dew or rain, can contaminate a picture as well. However, a trained photographic eye can usually rule out these things easily. This is especially the case when it comes to orbs caught on video. The manner of their behavior is sometimes truly mindboggling.

7. This photo was taken during a ghost tour at the haunted Grove Park Inn Resort and Spa in Asheville, North Carolina. A small orb appeared above the author's right hand, and a nebulous white mass appeared to his left side. *Photo courtesy Brian Irish*

Brian Irish is the current vice president and imaging expert for the L.E.M.U.R. (League of Energy Materialization and Unexplained phenomena Research) Paranormal Investigation Team, of which I'm founder and president. He has captured phenomenal footage of orbs displaying extraordinary characteristics. One night we were conducting an investigation of the 1889 WhiteGate Inn and Cottage, in Asheville, North Carolina. The old mansion served as a convalescent home for decades. There's even a melancholy room with bars on the window where a mentally unstable man was kept locked away . . . until he apparently killed himself. Our team was upstairs in the house observing an active bedroom. Brian rolled infrared-sensitive video as a bright orb emerged from a *closed* drawer, swept down to the right, and disappeared into another observer's stomach. The ball almost appeared supercharged at one point, glowing especially bright, displaying what could be a variance in energy level. These types of orbs are the truly paranormal ones. They can't be so easily explained away as simple mistakes and poor photography. Perhaps this footage shows an entity entering a person.

When it comes to the mystery of paranormal orbs, there are some theories that may explain their appearance. It is possible that the appearance of an entity can depend on its age. By "age," we mean the length of time it has been removed from a physical body.

Your etheric body closely resembles your physical one. In fact, one might go so far as to say it can look identical to your physical body. Once the physical is dead or destroyed, perhaps the energy body that initially leaves retains the shape of the physical form. This goes back to the phantom limb phenomenon. However, after enough time, could the boundaries of this shape break down? For example, look at a wall of dirt held back by a barrier. Once the barrier is removed, the mass of dirt can retain its shape, standing for some time. Given enough time to settle and erode, it will eventually fall down, released from its former container. This is why an older entity might sometimes appear as a mist or some other more abstract form as its energy breaks free of past, physical restrictions.

Ultimately, a free-floating energy form might take on the natural shape of balance—the sphere. When a soap bubble is blown from a ring, it is often misshapen at first. However, after wobbling a bit, it quickly turns into a sphere, due to surface tension. This is the most efficient and stable form for resisting extraneous energies. Each portion of the bubble is balanced. It is possible that an entity's energy structure could change the same way, eventually transforming from an unbalanced form to a perfect globe. If so, one could possibly gauge the age of a spirit by its appearance. Perhaps the more spherical the spirit seems, the older and more mature it may be.

There is one more refreshingly simple theory that may also explain orbs. Based on the corroboration of meters, it seems clear that many paranormal orbs carry a charge of static electricity. Perhaps an orb is invisible but its charge attracts tiny particles in the air, just like a charged comb attracts a small piece of paper. Maybe small airborne debris is naturally drawn into the electrical field of the orb, thereby emulating its shape and design. Such a fine and delicate conglomeration might be virtually invisible to the naked eye, but a camera's bright flash reflects it easily. In this fashion, orbs might indeed be caused by dust particles—particles that have adhered to an otherwise invisible form. If so, there should be a direct correlation between the number of particles in the air and the ease with which orbs are captured. The difficulty would lie in determining the difference between anomalies caused by random dust and those that represent a more advanced form.

In some cases, though a person may die old, his or her

apparition is seen as the younger self. How can this be? Here, another possible theory comes into play. If I now ask you to imagine a pink elephant with purple ears, you probably will visualize it mentally. In fact, the average human mind can visualize almost anything that can be described. Though you can see a pink elephant, that does not mean you can access it in any physical way. However, a ghost is not restricted to physical reality, as are living humans. Therefore, a spirit may be able to change its form at will. By visualizing a change in appearance, a specter may have the ability to choose how it is seen by others. If it can alter its energy structure, it may therefore be able to change the design to which ions will adhere. Maybe spirits are seen as mists and orbs in their "natural" physical state, but manipulate their appearance when dealing with living humans. This might also explain why ghosts don't always appear naked. Sometimes, clothes can be clearly observed on an apparition. Could this be a projection of what the entity wants to wear?

The electrical model can give us some sort of handle on understanding basic entity phenomena. However, the electrical model does not clearly explain how a spirit can make noises or create aromas. Sounds are the product of vibrations. Since ghosts could access physical force by means of static electricity, they could feasibly create vibrations. Some speculate that spirits may even form a larynx made of concentrated energy, capable of resonating air. Whether or not this is true, one must keep in mind that thunder, a powerful noise indeed, is created by electricity. The heat of lightning causes air currents to expand. When the expanding air collides with other fronts, they meet with a rumble. This is an indirect, yet realistic, way in which electricity can cause sound.

The issue of smells is even more complex. Witnesses are often alerted to the presence of a phantom by a specific aroma—a perfume, or cigar smoke, for example. A few months ago, I investigated a haunted property where smells were a significant part of the activity. Often, a "rotting" aroma would waft into the room. When a photograph was taken in conjunction, an anomaly would frequently appear in the picture. Perhaps these smells could be electrically initiated.

Strong ion concentrations do have a smell of their own. Static electricity in the air creates ozone. It has a refreshing and distinct odor. One can sometimes smell it right after an electrical storm. But it's hard to imagine how mere charges could duplicate a specific cologne. That goes for any of the distinct aromas people can experience when a spirit is around. The smells are usually something particular to the entity, and can make a strong impact on an observer who knew that entity in life and immediately recognizes the familiar aroma. If a ghostly smell is not the product of an *imprint* (as you'll see in the next section), it may be created by a direct mental link between the witness and the specter.

Sometimes, though a room is filled with people, only one person will see, hear, or smell a visiting ghost. That person is usually considered insane, of course. However, if indeed true, this might be due to a spiritual phenomenon that has far-reaching implications.

I'll never forget a somewhat chilling experience I observed while researching an old haunted house one crisp October night. I had never been to the home before, and I was accompanied by several friends. The owner of the location had been plagued with spectral phenomena for years. However, she herself was an enthusiast of paranormal activity. For her, the activity was a blessing.

Several of us were standing in a room at the base of a large staircase. We'd been there only a few minutes and were still engaged in introductions. Suddenly, one of the women in my group, Cindy, screamed. It scared the hell out of the rest of us, and before we could ask what was wrong, she was already out the door. I'm used to entering haunted locations with paranoid people who are uncomfortable and liable to flee over the smallest thing. I immediately figured that was the case with her: she'd probably seen a spider or something and gone berserk.

We all went outside to find Cindy in the yard, her face white and tears in her eyes. The owner of the house didn't seem surprised at all. She walked right up to Cindy and said, "You saw him, didn't you?"

"Yes! Yes!" was the reply.

After catching her breath and calming a bit, Cindy said she had looked at the bottom of the stairs and seen a frightening figure standing there. It was a priest, translucent in appearance, who had given her a sinister grin, then vanished. "Ah, you got to see the Monsignor!" exclaimed the owner. We were then told of how the property had once been a Catholic school, and how it was now haunted by the priest as well as a nun. That spot, at the bottom of the stairs, was where the apparition was most frequently seen. Lots of times, as one reached the first landing and turned to continue upward, the ghost would appear at the bottom, staring up at the individual with his infamous smile. Upon being seen, he would usually vanish.

The rest of us were unsure of how to view this incident. We were obviously impressed since Cindy had never before been to the location and had no knowledge of its activity. It was I who had brought these people to the property on my first trip there. And, just as I've described, I had no knowledge of the house's activity until Cindy's experience. On the other hand, we were all standing in the same area, looking roughly in the same direction, meeting the owner. I find it impossible for the phantom to have materialized in the said location without the rest of us having seen it. However, the owner said the priest is visible only to certain people sometimes, yet he is clearly interactive, usually acknowledging those who see him with a nod or a smile.

How could this be? How is it possible for one individual to witness blatant activity nonexistent to the rest of us? We can't simply write it off as a crazy person's imagination. If so, how did Cindy's imagination conjure up an experience consistent with those of others? We could simply say it was a hoax—that Cindy had been there before and was playing a trick on us. But there is absolutely no evidence to indicate this possibility. What other options do we have?

Just like you and me, an entity is at least partially composed of mental energy. That is to say, it apparently has a mind. Therefore, might it sometimes be able to communicate telepathically with an observer? Though, to the witness, the encounter appears completely external, it may in fact be contained within the observer's perception. Perhaps some spirits can bypass your physical senses, giving information to your brain directly. This would create a subjective experience, the kind that usually does little for science. I frequently hear stories about people being visited by spirits in their dreams. Is this encounter simply a fantastic dream, or is it easier for an entity to enter your mind when you're in a sleep state?

On the other hand, instead of an entity "beaming" a perception into your head, perhaps the key is the eye of the observer. In the section covering auras, we discussed the fact that not all people see the world in the same way. Some of us are color blind, while others can see colors the rest of us can't usually perceive. Are some people's eyes more capable of seeing the enigmatic frequency at which ghosts appear? Some psychics claim to be able to see and communicate with the dead based on this principle. If this phenomenon is valid, then some may be more receptive to the "other side." We know that other types of life on earth can see into realms invisible to humans. For instance, many insects can see ultraviolet light, especially bees. Like other earthly creatures, do some people have the ability to perceive more about the environment than most?

Regardless of whether the experience is due to a spirit's ability to project information or to an observer's ability to perceive it, one can sometimes have a private experience with an entity, even in the company of others. A spirit could transfer visions, thoughts, smells, tastes, sounds, or feelings this way. This is certainly a convenient theory, since it can explain how any ghostly experience, of any kind, might have a mechanism by which to manifest. From a scientist's perspective, this is also the dangerous quality of such a theory. If we can suddenly explain any ghost encounter as a subjective experience, that's little more than calling it a hallucination (an illusion created by the observer's mind). However, we know spirits have objective, empirical, documentable qualities.

As you'll see later, we can record ghostly manifestations in photographs, on audio tapes, via energy field detectors, and a number of other means. All these instruments record objective information. When used efficiently, they can provide evidence that proves ghostly activity does occur. We can't prove that each manifestation represents some form of life after death. However, it's possible that such evidence may *eventually* lead to incontrovertible proof of an afterlife.

Regardless of how spectral energies can influence an observer's perception, it is always necessary to focus on gaining the empirical evidence. Otherwise, your experience is just another ghost story. Though it might be a good one, it'll be a much more valuable one with proper documentation. Besides, it's possible that your senses will perceive one thing while the equipment perceives another.

Ghost hunters often develop photographs and find pictures

of phantoms that were invisible when the photos were taken. Just as the camera is able to capture something the eyes could not, it's likely that even when you *do* see a ghost, it will appear somehow different in a photograph. Like all reality, the ghost-encounter experience is a combination of an objective and subjective experience. What looks like a mist might appear as orbs in a photo. What resembles a solid woman to the naked eye might yield an arc of light in a photo. It's a shame that we can't always document the subjective experience in the same way as the objective. Perhaps future technology will change that. However, for the time being, focus on where it counts the most.

As you can see, trying to understand conscious ghostly activity is a complex matter. The challenge starts with the fact that you're dealing with a being just as intelligent as you. This being has its own free will and personal strength. Just because a spirit can interact with the living does not mean it will. The psychology of entities is just as intricate and mysterious as the psychology of living persons. Also, it seems clear that some spirits are stronger than others. Strength may come from their sheer size, age, composition, or mastery of breaching the gap between the etheric and the physical. Whatever the case, some specters are more capable of interacting with us than others. Next, for some experiences, the environmental conditions have to be right, with a proper atmosphere for manipulating charges. Then, even once the spirit materializes, we have the task of sifting through the relationship between objective and subjective evidence.

To be an effective ghost researcher, you must be a logical, analytical thinker who can take many variables, both known and unknown, and deduce how they interrelate. As your investigations proceed, you'll begin to see patterns of activity emerge, such as consistency among weather conditions. Just keep in mind, whenever you encounter a ghost, the more information you can record about that experience, the greater your chances of progressing your understanding. Of all types of ghostly occurrences, it seems entities are the most prevalent. At the same time, they can be the most difficult to understand.

TYPES OF ENTITIES

So far, this chapter has shown you how living, organic beings might still be able to exist without a physical shell. We've focused on the ghosts of humans. However, it seems animal entities manifest in the same way. I frequently hear of encounters with ghost dogs or cats. Those who see them say they appear and behave just like living animals. However, they are often translucent, and their locomotion is under-standably more fluid. As with most ghosts, they are seen for a few seconds until simply disappearing.

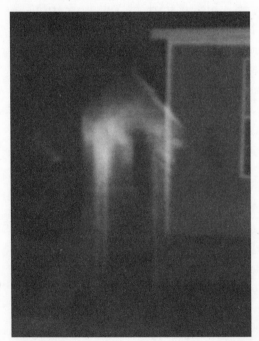

8. A horse apparition? *Photo copyright © 2001 by Lynn Jackson/Lillian Ritch.*

One of the most interesting paranormal photos I've ever seen was taken on a haunted farm in Lancaster, South Carolina. One day, a completely healthy horse dropped dead without explanation. The family buried him near the house. A short time afterward, a photograph was taken in the area. When it was developed, the clear apparition of the horse appeared (Illus. 8).

When we think of animal entities, we shouldn't restrict ourselves to just cats, dogs, owls, wolves, and other creatures of traditional superstition. I have even visited locations where dinosaur ghosts were reported. According to biologists, the organisms on earth right now are only a tiny fraction of all species that ever existed. There are surely millions of animals that once lived that we have never seen. Even dinosaurs were not discovered until the 1800s, even though their remains have always been available to man. How many other species left no bones or traces for us to find? People sometimes report seeing ghostly entities that don't appear human but certainly look different from any known animal. Could these be ghosts of unfamiliar creatures of the past?

It can be confusing, trying to understand how to categorize spiritual entities, but the situation can become even more complex as ghosts may sometimes have the ability to travel through what we perceive as time.

In *The Field Guide to Ghosts and Other Apparitions*, Hilary Evans and Patrick Huyghe devote some thought to organizing ghosts into past, present, and future categories. If you want to explore that area more, I recommend their book. However, here is a basic breakdown of each type of spirit.

Ghosts of the Past: These are the ones with which you're most familiar. We usually talk about ghosts of the past when addressing entities. *Revenant* is a term for an entity that comes back only a few times after death. It might be a spirit who's procrastinating about moving on, or one who wants to accomplish some quick goals—tie up a few loose ends—before leaving the physical plane. You might think of a *haunter* as a ghost that sticks around for decades, centuries, or even longer.

Ghosts of the Present: When exploring ghosts, we're usually talking about the paranormal remnant of someone or something that no longer exists in the physical plane. However, sometimes the ghost of a *living person* is seen. This is an extremely rare occurrence, though. This text has explored what may happen when the etheric body leaves behind the dead physical body. But it seems the etheric body can sometimes leave the living physical body behind, returning later to carry on life as usual.

For thousands of years, reports have surfaced regarding the out-of-body experience, or OBE. According to those who say they've experienced it, they are often able to look down and see their physical bodies sleeping below. They now occupy a translucent body, completely weightless, that can be controlled by thought, called the "etheric body." However, in this context, it's often called the "astral body." Using the astral body, they can fly anywhere in the world like a superhero, passing through physical matter. In fact, they claim the skies are filled with other astral travelers. Sometimes, people speak of suddenly finding themselves out of body unexpectedly and spontaneously. Others claim they can control the technique, and do it at will. This is called "astral projection."

I have had lengthy discussions with an elderly man named James Wright, who claims he used to be an avid astral traveler. Almost every night, he would lie in bed, close his eyes, and eventually enter a deep meditative state. He couldn't explain how he reached this state, but considered it a natural gift.

Eventually, James would rise out of his body to find himself hovering above the bed. At that point, he would fly away, the galaxy at his disposal.

He began his adventures by traveling to Europe. He'd hover over a street corner for hours and hours, just watching people walk by and go about their business, completely oblivious to his invisible presence. Over a period of years, he visited each part of the earth he wanted to see, then set out to reach the moon! He finally stopped astral projection because of a disturbing experience he had. He floated into a friend's house one night and found his friend's wife in bed with another lover. James was tortured over whether he should tell his friend. The experience made him realize that it wasn't right for him to invade other people's privacy, even with his gift. It made him wonder about the ethics of astral projection altogether. He was also concerned as to whether some other entity might be able to possess his body while he was away. All in all, he figured he'd have plenty of time to float around after his death, so he vowed to literally keep himself on the ground.

Stories like James's are not all that uncommon. Over the years, I've met at least a dozen people who claimed to have had some sort of OBE. One can imagine his or her ghost leaving while the body is able to maintain its mechanical living functions. Sometimes—again, extremely rarely—these apparitions of living people are apparently seen, usually for a very brief period, no more than a few seconds. Such is especially the case if there's a crisis situation. Remember the possible telepathic connection between parents and children? This might be a similar phenomenon: Sometimes, if a child is in a serious accident, the child's apparition will appear, in a flash of stress, to the parents. It can even happen the other way around, the parents appearing to the child. It's almost as if, for a second, one person leaves his or her body, usually involuntarily, to reach out to another for help. These types of Ghosts of the Present are usually brief visits from a loved one at a time of emergency or death.

There are also cases where a person's "phantom double" appears. For example, in 1845, thirteen students in Latvia watched their teacher, Emilie Sagee, working on a blackboard. Suddenly, there was an exact duplicate of her, working alongside her in an identical fashion. The teacher was oblivious to the occurrence. The double looked like her in every way, including clothing, except it held no chalk. After a few moments, the two figures merged into one woman again.

A "doppelganger" encounter is similar to that of seeing a double. However, it's usually called a doppelganger if the double is not engaged in the same actions. An author once told me he was walking down a street in New York when he had the most shocking experience of his life. At one point, he casually glanced up to see himself walking toward himself! His doppelganger looked just like him and even wore the same clothes. However, it seemed just as shocked to see him as he was to see it. They stared at each other for a moment, then the apparition disappeared.

On an even stranger level, there are cases of people engaged in the most mundane of activities—doing the dishes, brushing their teeth, etc.—who look up and see a living friend or loved one standing there. After a second or two, the figure disappears. Upon calling the person whose apparition was seen, it's discovered that everything is fine. There is no explanation for why this occurs.

Apparitions of living people—Ghosts of the Present—are difficult to study. Manifestations of this category usually happen only once. A ghost hunter should be aware of their existence, but should also keep in mind that they have little relevance to most ghost investigations.

Ghosts of the Future: Like Ghosts of the Present, these entities usually only appear once. A basic example would be when people see apparitions of themselves or someone they know who appears to be older than that person currently is. However, most of the time, a spirit from the future is carrying a message to inform the observer of future events. This type of phantom is known as a "harbinger." It usually appears to bring a warning.

Nursing home staff members report harbingers on a regular basis. Just before someone is about to die, they often see figures near the person. Sometimes, a dark, robed phantom, looking quite literally like the grim reaper, will appear. At other times, winged specters glide silently down the hall toward a patient's room.

Harbingers can also prevent death. In one case, a businessman told me of being awakened in the night by the spirit of his dead father. The apparition told him and his wife to get up and leave immediately. They soon realized their house was ablaze. If it were not for the warning, they would have surely died. Strangely enough, what seemed to be a Ghost from the Past, his dead father, came to warn him of future tragedy.

When the average layman thinks of a ghost, he or she thinks of an entity. This is because the majority of ghostly activity, approximately 60–70 percent, is the product of an entity.

In order to identify an entity, remember its qualities:

Entities:
1. Are conscious beings.
2. Are usually humans or animals who have died.
3. Often use the electrical environment to manifest.
4. Can create both objective and subjective experiences.
5. Can come from the past, present, or future.

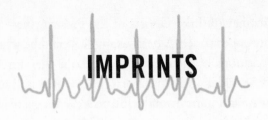

IMPRINTS

Entities are usually some remnant of a living creature. However, what about the ghosts of inanimate objects? A classic example is *The Flying Dutchman,* an ominous ghost ship. For nearly two centuries, it has brought misfortune to those who see it.

According to legend, the cruel captain of the ship was a tough and fearless man. When he and his crew sailed the majestic vessel around the Cape of Good Hope, below the southern tip of Africa, a dark, terrifying storm swept in, and the frightened crew pleaded with their captain, begging him to sail into a safe harbor. The captain was drunk and boisterous. He laughed at the howling winds and crashing waves, then grinned madly as he screamed to God: "You haven't the power to sink my ship!" Not surprisingly, it went down.

To this day, *The Flying Dutchman* is still seen sailing the restless waters. As a storm brews, she emerges, as from a mist, then glides across the dark sea, her spectral luminescence glowing all around her. Then, the ship fades into the unclear distance. If one beholds this sight, it is believed he should dock immediately.

This ship is obviously what we would consider a nonconscious thing. In fact, as far as we're concerned, it never had consciousness or life to begin with. You can see how an apparition like this conflicts with our ideas about entities. Granted, all objects, even ships, have an electromagnetic energy body. But if we're talking about nothing more than an "energy ship" that can float around just like a physical one, why doesn't it float away or come ashore? Why is it always seen in the same general area under the same general conditions, sailing the same general way?

Sometimes ghosts do not appear conscious. They are completely oblivious to observers, and always look and act *the same*—almost like a recording being played back. In fact, the phenomenon is really no different from a grand-scale short film. They lack the sense of spontaneity and interaction found with an entity.

For example, if a heinous murder takes place in the bedroom of a house, for years thereafter, witnesses may see that specific murder replayed in that bedroom. Each incident would be identical, and the murderer and victim would not behave as though being observed. It's as if the event made an impression upon the environment that is somehow recorded.

I have been to several locations haunted by Native American spirits. I myself have heard the low beat of Indian drums that drifts in at night. In fact, my team has even been able to record this phenomenon. For countless years, the drumbeats have resounded in the hills and valleys. Now, is their spiritual rhythm literally impressed upon the area? At some times—the *right* times—does it emerge again?

When it seems that a significant or persistent event has imprinted the environment, this is called, fittingly enough, an IMPRINT. Since it's almost as if the location has some sort of memory, some researchers also refer to this phenomenon as a "place memory haunting" or "place residue haunting." In fact, some parapsychologists use only the term *haunting* or *haunted* to describe this phenomenon. You should note that, in this book, "haunted" or "haunting" are used in their most general sense, applied to both psychic imprints and conscious-entity activity. For us, a haunted location is one where ghostly activity, of whatever kind, persists for a period of more than a year.

Imprints are almost always seen, and sometimes heard. In rare cases, an imprint can be felt as well. That is to say, if you see the imprint of a vehicle speeding toward you, it will usually pass right through you. On the other hand, there is a chance it will *not* pass right through you. In some cases, an imprint is more than just an audio/visual experience. If so, you could be harmed. An actual physical presence can be reproduced when the imprint plays. Though it's convenient to think of an imprint as a naturally recorded short film, you must keep in mind that this film is capable of recording some or all aspects of a realistic, full-scale, three-dimensional experience. However, they only replay for a few seconds, up to a minute, and are seen only when some unknown conditions are right. Even an "anniversary imprint," one that is seen around a certain time each year, is not always dependable. Some observers see them while others do not. Whether or not one experiences an imprint evidently depends on at least one of two factors: the observer's perception, or the conditions under which the images are seen. These recorded acts might replay themselves only when certain environmental factors are present. They therefore might be influenced by the presence of electrostatic ions, the earth's magnetic shifts, weather patterns, or any number of currently unknown variables. This would mean that virtually anyone could witness them if the conditions were right. On the other hand, the ability to witness psychic imprints may instead reside in the eye of the beholder. If this information is retained in a form that only some people can see or experience, then an observer who unwittingly possesses this ability might be stunned to observe an incident that others do not or cannot.

But why would an episode imprint itself on the environment? And how? Albert Einstein once said: "The distinction between past, present, and future is only an illusion, however persistent." Keeping these words in mind, let's explore the concept of time, itself.

Humans are able to efficiently travel and organize our lives by dividing the planet in many ways. We establish grid lines of latitude and longitude. We create time zones, which lead to measurable days and weeks. However, grid lines and time zones are the invention of mankind. We took a vast reality and used our imaginations to divide it into manageable portions of reference. Because we all agree to visualize the planet in the same way, we are all able to coordinate our lives more effectively. However, simply because this way of viewing the planet serves its purpose, do not become lulled into believing it accurately describes reality. It provides a precise way to describe man's perception of reality, but that does not mean it accounts for how it actually appears and functions. There are no literal lines drawn on the planet! Though science is a quest for truth, it does not always indicate truth; it merely gives us explanations that agree with the observations.

When we see a volcano, we could assume it starts at the surface, since that's all we truly perceive. We could effectively deal with them by simply staying away from them. Reaching this conclusion takes no more than a "surface observation." However, though the surface plays a definite and easily observed role, that does not mean one could achieve a complete understanding of volcanoes without exploring deep within the earth. You must use this same line of thinking when addressing the concept of time. The perception of time is the most mysterious of all human experiences, and we have agreed to view it as a single, irrevocable line of events because that model usually corresponds with our experience. But does that model accurately represent the full design and implications of time, or perhaps only the surface?

To the practical mind, it seems the past is literally gone forever—reduced to a mere memory. But what is the past? The idea of a past and a future is dependent upon the existence of the present. After all, the present is all that divides past from future. Without the present, past and future suddenly have no meaning. But what is the present? How do we define the present? In order to exist, the present must occupy a finite position in our linear concept of time. Therefore, how long does the present last? A second? It couldn't last a second, because even a second has a beginning and an end, and a span in between. That would mean we'd have a past and future *within* our past and future. This obviously does not make sense. So, does the present last a half-second, then? Even this won't work because, again, a half-second also has a beginning and an end. In fact, we could never come up with a measurement for the present, regardless of how small, that does not have a beginning and end. Therefore, if the present does not, indeed *cannot*, begin or end, then it does not exist in any literal, definable way!

There is clearly a difference between existence and our perception of existence. Many concepts are the invention of mankind, such as the calendar, time, music, and so on. In order to live pragmatically productive lives, humans must divide, categorize, and label nature. However, nature does not always agree with our labels—hence the need for leap years (and even leap seconds). "Leap events" occur when our linear cloaks fall short of covering the subject beneath. In order to compensate, we must throw on a patch here and there. We know our current way of dicing reality into time is inaccurate; otherwise, there would be no need for "leaps." The same phenomenon can be viewed in many different ways, just as we can define the same temperature in Celsius or Fahrenheit. Is our current view of time, as a one-way street, too limited?

If you get on a spaceship and travel around the earth at nearly 186,000 miles per second (the speed of light) for a year, you would return to earth to find that everyone else had aged by *two* years. If you don't understand Einstein's Theory of Special Relativity, this might sound absurd. However, in 1971, an exercise was conducted to test this principle: the so-called Hafele-Keating experiment. The U.S. Naval Observatory took two atomic clocks and synchronized them down to billionths of a second. One was kept stationary in Washington, D.C. while the other was placed on a jet. The aircraft flew around the world and then the clocks were compared. Just as predicted, the one on the ground was approximately fifty-billionths of a second faster than the one on the jet. At such attainable speeds, the time variation was extremely tiny, but the possibility of time travel had been proven. This showed that time is a flexible thing; as one moves faster, it slows. Time changes with regard to the observer and his or her conditions. The only reason we haven't yet built a time machine is that we don't have the technology to reach the kind of speeds, and withstand the kind of forces, necessary.

Our idea of the past, present, and future is based upon our unique perspective on life. Time to a human is not necessarily consistent with time to an insect, microorganism, or alien. My present can be your past, and vice versa. Time is a fluid thing. When Einstein says the distinction between past, present, and future is only an illusion, this is apparently what he means.

In daily life, we use the term *present* loosely. It can describe the day, the hour, the moment, or even an entire era. It can be used loosely because it has no true definition. If something cannot be defined, does it exist? If there is no true present—and hence no past or future—then all time is actually taking place at once; we are simply experiencing it one moment at a time. This is certainly a complex idea because it is so foreign to our usual way of thinking about the universe and how we experience it. This idea conjures up even more complex issues, like predeterminism and destiny.

Remember the mind-body dilemma? Another classic philosophical debate is the conflict between freedom and determinism. Through a series of mental experiments, I just explained how "the present" does not exist in a literal way. If there is no present, and all reality is taking place at once, that means the future has already occurred. This would represent a *deterministic* view: the future is predetermined. This should explain concepts like fate and destiny, that unavoidable events *will* occur, out of our control. A strict Newtonian perspective views all existence as nothing more than a chain reaction between particles. It can imply that reality behaves like billiard balls on a table: if you could know the *exact* angle, power, and motion of the cue ball as it hit, you could predict the course and destination of each other ball. In the same sense, if you knew the exact variable of each particle of matter in the Big Bang, could you predict the entire course of history? Some people have a significant problem with this idea.

If everything is determined, that means you have no choice in life, which in turn means you suddenly have no freedom. This doesn't seem to make sense, though, since you can jump off a cliff at any time. Surely this represents a kind of freedom, right? On the other hand, even though you *could* jump off that cliff, you're not going to, are you? So maybe it was predetermined for you *not* to do so. Besides, how can something like freedom exist scientifically? Freedom requires independence and spontaneity, but those concepts require an effect without a cause. How can that be? You can see the natural paradoxes that arise. The greatest mysteries are those we perceive as paradoxes. You may as well ask: What is infinity? Whether life operates in a free or deterministic way, or according to some combination of the two, the implications of this debate could fill up an entire book. However, we won't linger on them in this one.

If the past, present, and future are separated by nothing more than our subjective perception, then it is possible that "past" events are always occurring simultaneously with "present" events. If so, then perhaps they can sometimes be observed. However, only certain past events can be seen as imprints, and they're usually of a negative nature. But why would something tragic, like a murder, "replay" instead of something benevolent? The answer may lie in the emotional intensity of the episode.

When humans kill, either themselves or others, an enormous amount of emotional energy is expended. This is especially the case in battles. In the American Civil War, there were days when thousands of men slaughtered one another in a matter of minutes. When energy is expended under especially stressful conditions, this energy may create a stronger and more distinct impression than that created by less-forceful incidents, especially if the environment is electromagnetically sensitive, like an audio tape. Does the environment possess some ability to record those events that transpire within it? If so, then a high-powered incident may imprint it more powerfully and distinctly. Maybe all events that take place at a given location are recorded there in some way. However, we currently lack the means to access most of those recordings. On the other hand, especially powerful ones are most easily observed. If we can understand exactly what gives us the ability to see them, maybe we could one day access all of them! An audio tape recording fades with time. Do imprints do the same?

If all time is indeed taking place at once, the future should be as accessible as the past. If there are *many* possible futures, then at least one of them could be accessible. Perhaps this is why some psychics and prophets are able to see things to come. Their perceptions may allow them to see into the future (or at least *a* future) via seeing psychic imprints of the past.

We know, according to relativity, that we should be able to travel through time if we could attain the appropriate speed. With our current technology, it may be physically impossible. But what about the mind? We don't know exactly what thoughts are. However, they can manifest instantly and, if telepathy is genuine, they can travel in some sense. It is possible that thoughts might be able to attain the speed necessary for *mental* time travel.

If one can psychically see the future, it's called "precognition." Might this be achieved by sending thoughts "out" and into the future? Even though we can't currently create a machine that can do this, it might certainly be possible for a mind. On the other hand, some people claim an ability to psychically see things that occurred in the past. This is called "retrocognition." Unlike a traditional ghost encounter, where the manifestations appear to be objective, those who experience retrocognition or precognition generally know they are having a private and self-contained experience. Collectively, you could call someone with these abilities "clairvoyant."

The human mind is arguably the most amazing thing in the observed universe. We are not separate from nature and the universe, but instead an intimate part of it. Can some minds overcome extreme physical barriers? Can *all* minds do this from time to time?

Aside from delving into mysterious theories about what time may be, we must also look at some practical developments that might change our view of passing events.

Advanced audio technicians say we already have the technology to record conversations that took place hours or days before at any given location. When you speak, all you actually project are vibrations. The other person's ears interpret the waves as sound. However, the vibrations that create sounds do not always dissolve immediately. Sometimes they continue to bounce around an area long after they've been transferred into sound by an ear. By making extremely slow recordings in a location, then playing them back at an ultrahigh speed, these sound waves can be restored to their original speed. As you can imagine, such technology is of particular value to the law enforcement community.

Television and radio station personnel speak of a strange phenomenon in the world of broadcasting. According to them, there have been notable incidents where television or radio shows, broadcast decades before, could be picked up and experienced like new. The broadcast waves can bounce around in the ionosphere for many years before dissolving. This could be similar to how the environment might hold the resonant frequencies of an intense past event.

The previous two examples do not represent a speculative model of time and reality. Instead, they are based upon familiar activity—the behavior of electromagnetic waves. Though they are not the product of "time travel" in a literal sense, they still provide a means by which some event that occurred in the past might still be detectable in a future environment. Could the imprint phenomenon be a more complex version of this? Or is it caused by time principles too advanced for our understanding? Perhaps the explanation for imprints resides somewhere between the two.

One more amazing example involves Walter Gibson, a well-known magician and writer who lived in New York. Using the pen name Maxwell Grant, he is best known for having authored the crime-fighter series *The Shadow*. The clandestine, swashbuckling hero was immortalized by a successful radio show and comics in the 1930s and a major motion picture, starring Alec Baldwin, in 1994. Gibson was an intense man, with an overwhelming sense of concentration. He wrote 283 *Shadow* books, and he could write a full novel in less than a week.

For a period, he holed himself up in a Greenwich Village studio and churned out an extraordinary number of books in only a few months. During that period, he expended an overwhelming amount of energy imagining his characters in vivid detail. For years afterward, future residents of the cottage claimed it was haunted by his characters. They would look down a hall to see The Shadow turn a corner, his cape billowing, or watch a frantic villain flee. It was as if Gibson's thoughts had been so powerful and concentrated, they created an imprint that took on some objective quality. Perhaps time and reality are so malleable that some of us can impress it with our thoughts alone.

Regardless of exactly how time functions, paranormal imprints show us that, for whatever reason, events can be recorded in an environment. When they occur, there is a disturbance in the electromagnetic environment, very similar to what occurs when an entity manifests. In fact, it seems that imprints usually materialize in a fashion identical to that of an entity—by manipulating electrostatic charges and EMFs to appear as a plasma. Of course, the energies created by an entity are capable of moving about in an erratic or spontaneous fashion. The energy of an imprint displays patterns over a period of time since it's the same thing happening over and over. As you'll see later, the equipment currently used to study entities and imprints is the same. Telling the difference between the two depends on your keen observation. Of course, with an imprint, the location's history may play a more important role as well. An entity can move about, but an imprint stays at the place where it was made. Keep in mind that one location can have numerous imprints, but each individual imprint will always behave the same basic way. Any variance in an imprint, from manifestation to manifestation, could reflect a change in environmental conditions, wearing down with age, or an alteration of some other unknown variable.

You've seen that entities can apparently come from the past, present, or future. It's possible that they transcend time according to principles similar to those demonstrated by imprints. You might even find that places where imprints occur are more conducive to seeing an entity. Whatever electromagnetic anomaly is at work, it's a key factor in experiencing ghosts. Remember, both entities and imprints are ghosts, just different kinds. Given enough observation, you can easily tell the difference.

If ghostly activity is unpredictable, erratic, spontaneous, and interactive, it is probably the work of a conscious entity. If it is predictable, redundant, and oblivious to observers and changed surroundings, it is most likely an imprint.

Imprints:
1. Are nonconscious.
2. Can appear as human, animal, plant, or as inanimate objects.
3. Display no interaction with observers.
4. Replay in an identical way each time.
5. Stay in the same location.
6. Often use the electrical environment to manifest.
7. Can create both objective and subjective experiences.

WARPS

Many traditional ghost investigators study only entities and imprints, which are the basis of 90 percent of location hauntings. However, we shall now delve into the fringes of paranormal research. Let's begin with the most complex of them all.

If a location is haunted by an entity, certain earmarks are exhibited. The activity will be spontaneous, erratic, and interactive. If it's an imprint, it will be nonconscious, predictable, and oblivious. Sometimes, you might find a place with both. But what if you find a place that includes not only both these types of activity, but even more?

My team and I investigated a property where an overwhelming number of paranormal occurrences had been reported. There were conscious entities who would physically assault the owners, leaving distinct bruises and cuts. Parts of the house, and vehicles on the property, would suddenly burst into flame without explanation. Often, visitors became sick or suffered from surprising attacks of aches and pains. A barrage of imprints pulsated around the grounds, and the owners had captured thousands of anomalous images on video and in stills. There was even a time when someone in the house turned to find herself staring into what appeared to be another dimension: a horrific and surreal place, with swirling clouds and disturbing activity. Then, it vanished. Small objects, like silverware and ink pens, would transport themselves to other locations. All in all, any kind of ghostly manifestation was possible, sometimes occurring by way of extreme and negative synchronicity.

So far, the activity we've covered is caused primarily by extraordinary events that may have affected any location. However, it sometimes seems like the location *itself* has something to do with the ghostly activity. The earth is not a perfect sphere. In fact, it's shaped sort of like a pear. Because of this, it wobbles on its path of orbit. Basically, it's far from a perfectly balanced body in space. The earth's magnetic field corresponds with the planet's physical form. Since the earth is not balanced, neither is its field. It therefore seems logical that some places on the planet are subjected to unusual geomagnetic activity, greater or lesser than the rest of the earth. This doesn't even take into consideration the magnetic fields caused by physical stress on fault lines (see the chapter Naturals). Different parts of the surface are also affected in a unique way based upon their position in relation to the sun. The sun hurls massive bursts of radiation at the earth, and some places are more, or less, affected by that as well.

There are places on earth where the laws of physics seem to be distorted, and reality sometimes behaves in unfamiliar ways, creating ghostly effects. This type of location is what we call a WARP. These are rare, but once one is located, it usually becomes popular in a hurry. People are thrilled by the idea of going to a location where almost *anything* can happen. One of the world's most popular warps is the Bermuda Triangle.

Thinking of the Bermuda Triangle usually conjures up images of sinking ships and falling planes. Indeed, since 1900, more than one thousand people have disappeared over those waters between Bermuda, Florida, and Puerto Rico. Even more compelling than the number of disappearances is the way they manifest. For example, consider the five navy planes that vanished at the same time on December 5, 1945. A mayday was sent from the leader: "We cannot see land . . . everything is wrong . . . strange. We can't be sure of our position. We seem to be lost. Even the sea doesn't look as it should." Contact was then lost and a rescue plane was sent out immediately. It, too, promptly disappeared. No trace of the six planes has been found to this day.

Pilots frequently report instrument interference in the area, like compasses spinning. In addition, mysterious streaks and balls of light are seen flitting about certain areas. The first person to record seeing these illuminations was Christopher Columbus in 1492. He wrote about them in his log. There is no shortage of ghostly tales in the area, including apparitions, imprints, and "time slips."

In the 1980s, Rick Stratton, a television crew technician in his twenties, and a friend rented a cottage deep in the New England countryside. The secluded house was built by Moravian settlers in the 1800s. He enjoyed living there for several weeks and experienced nothing out of the usual. One night, he walked into the kitchen to get a drink. When he stepped through the doorway, he was immediately shocked. The kitchen looked completely different. The entire room appeared "old-fashioned." But, strangest of all, a man sat at the table eating, and a woman stood over the sink. They were both dressed in antiquated garb. The old man and woman looked at Rick and their eyes popped wide in surprise, as though they were seeing a ghost. Rick stared at them for a few seconds, each person speechless. Then, they vanished, and the kitchen was back to normal.

This kind of experience isn't a simple entity case. That's because the entire room was different. It isn't an imprint, since the man and woman were conscious of the observer and reacted to his presence. So, where does that leave us? This is the type of phenomenon we would call a "time slip." This means that it seemed like two moments in time, one in the 1800s and one in the late 1900s, slipped and merged together for a brief period. Such phenomena can take place at a warp location. You can see why it's still classified as ghostly—it demonstrates activity that allows us to observe some remnant of the past, or at least think we might be.

Warps exemplify the most complicated issues facing science today. These are places where reality is not just affected by an anomaly, but that reality itself is behaving in an anomalous way. They can distort all our ideas about how reality functions. Up can become down, and inside can become outside. Time stops, reverses, plunges forward, or has no sense of direction at all. You can hallucinate, or find that the environment around you has changed for an unmeasurable period. There can be an unbelievable amount of electromagnetic energy, or surprisingly no energy at all. Basically, warps are amorphous hot spots of ghostly phenomena and paranormal activity in general.

It is difficult to define warps, since the range of their manifestations can be completely foreign and unpredictable. They're sort of a paranormal catchall. For that reason, it's easy for some to frown upon them. They are difficult to define. Warps are not active all the time, and the conditions necessary to trigger their activity is a mystery.

Warps are often filled with entities—sometimes hundreds or thousands of them. Possibly by distorting space/time, warps may create natural *portals*. These are "doorways" through which an entity might be able to materialize, or gain some kind of physical access, more easily. Generally, these entities are also able to manufacture more strength due to the "thinned veil."

It is rare to find a strong warp. However, if you do, it can provide a lifetime of research material. Oftentimes, sacred locations are thought to be warps, especially those chosen by the ancient Celts and Egyptians. Some even believe pyramids were built to *create* warps. The idea is that such structures, by nature of their design, manipulate energies. You may have heard of "pyramid power." Throughout history, various inventors and manufacturers have claimed you can sharpen a dull razor blade by placing it beneath a cardboard pyramid. Plants beneath the shape are said to grow fuller, and stored meat decomposes more slowly. Hanging a cardboard pyramid over your bed is thought to incite vivid dreams.

Whatever the case, our planet is, in many ways, superior to our technology. Capacitors (devices to store, strengthen, and manipulate electrical charges) were not "invented" until 1745, when German scientist Ewald Georg von Kleist developed the earliest Leyden jar. However, for billions of years, the earth has been a natural capacitor. The ground is one electrode, the upper atmosphere another, and the space between is an insulator. Life on earth was solar powered long before Einstein's explanation of the photoelectric effect. Again and again, we find ourselves mimicking nature, but patting ourselves on the back as if the concept were original to humans. On the other hand, there are still lots of amazing phenomena produced by nature that man has never learned to duplicate for practical purposes. You will appreciate this concept even more after reading the upcoming chapter Naturals.

You may have read about black holes. These are areas of mass so dense that not even light can escape. For years, black holes were considered imaginary. Now, scientists are confident that they do indeed exist. Famed theoretical physicist Stephen Hawking has written about what is now called Hawking Radiation. This is an emanation of energy that might indicate the presence of a black hole. It is based on the idea that some particles *can* escape a black hole—those hurled back into space as the black hole slowly dissolves over time. Within a black hole is a point called a "singularity." This is the spot at which the known laws of science break down and do not apply.

Is it possible that, *sometimes, some* kind of limited, singularity-type phenomenon might exist at *some* places on earth? Usually, ghostly activity concerns an aspect of the past that still plays a paranormal role in the future. A warp is a place that can essentially blur the distinctions of past, present, and future. When you find one, be prepared for anything.

Warps are:
1. Areas where the conventional laws of physics can break down.
2. Places where linear time does not always apply.
3. Locations infested with entities, imprints, and a barrage of other paranormal activity.
4. Unpredictable areas that can twist perceptions beyond the understanding of logic.

POLTERGEIST ACTIVITY

The word *poltergeist* is German. The verb *polter* means "noisy" and *geist* means "ghost." Therefore, we have a "noisy ghost." This refers to the rambunctious behavior of an assumed entity. However, the meaning of this term has changed with time.

Traditionally, poltergeists were thought to be mischievous spirits who enjoyed frightening people and pulling pranks. They have always been most notable for being *extremely* interactive with the physical environment, always moving and throwing objects, popping bottle tops, flickering lights, making loud noises, and the like. In addition, poltergeists have always been considered the most cruel and showmanlike of ghosts, apparently enjoying the shock of witnesses. At first, activity of this kind sounds like a paranormal researcher's dream. However, the devil is always in the details.

In the early to mid-1900s, as researchers spent more time pursuing this type of activity, they began to notice some puzzling things about it. For one thing, although so much ghostly activity took place, and it seemed that some invisible entity was influencing the environment, the presumed entity was usually not seen. Also, unlike a traditional haunting, the phenomenon was temporary (usually a few days to a few months). But, most significant of all was the fact that it seemed to center around one individual, called an "agent." Though anyone *can* be an agent, in most cases it was an adolescent female. This eventually led researchers to develop new theories about what poltergeist activity may be.

Adolescent females go through extreme hormonal changes. Because of this, they expend a great deal of emotional energy. It is often a confusing, bleak, and frustrating time for a young woman. It seemed possible that a poltergeist was a mysterious entity that fed off this energy, drawing it in and then expelling it into the environment. Perhaps the spirit stuck around for a limited time, using the surplus energy while it was available. However, it seemed more likely that a poltergeist was not an entity at all. This is especially due to the fact that an entity is almost never seen. If telekinesis, the ability to directly control the environment with thoughts, is genuine, it may be a suppressed human ability. That being the case, it appeared possible that these young women subconsciously released their pent-up frustrations in telekinetic bursts of energy. Therefore, they themselves would have had no idea they were causing the activity. Once the climactic period of hormonal stress and mental tension had passed, the activity would cease. Is it possible that these girls would grow into adults with a higher propensity for telekinetic ability?

For decades now, paranormal researchers have required poltergeist activity to meet a specific set of standards. The activity would be temporary, centered around an agent, and focus on disturbance of physical objects. This way of viewing poltergeist activity has served its purpose well. However, as time has gone on, and researchers have been able to study even more phenomena, it seems the definition should be broadened a bit. Maybe this traditional scenario is only one part of a larger category. For our purposes, we shall now redefine the term: Whenever the repeated manifestation of ghostly activity is primarily dependent upon the presence of a specific individual or individuals, it is POLTERGEIST ACTIVITY.

At a house haunted by entities, we should usually be able to set up a camera in the place, leave the property, and record phenomena in the empty house. Sure, the entities may not be as active as they are when someone is around, but they still possess the ability to influence the environment, and that ability is not limited by who is present. Likewise, we should be able to capture imprint activity when no one is around. The same can be said for most warp phenomena. However, whatever poltergeist activity is, be it the product of an entity that is using the agent's energy, or a subconscious telekinetic power of the agent, it is primarily dependent upon the agent's physical presence. This is the only category of ghostly phenomena that is specifically dependent on a human presence.

Indeed, as in the traditional understanding, most agents are female. And it's true that adolescent females going through hormonal changes are the usual suspects. Most of the time, this activity does not last more than a few months. However, in rare cases, it manifests spontaneously throughout someone's entire lifetime. The occurrences can even cease for years, then return one day. Though it's possible that an entity is responsible for this activity, this is probably not the case, since one is rarely seen, and the effects don't unveil "personality traits" over time.

Most of the time, ghostly phenomena manifest by subtle yet distinct occurrences. Some of it takes place in such a quiet and controlled way, you might not notice it until after the fact. This is often the case when objects are displaced. It's common for residents of a haunted house to find, much to their surprise, that items in the home have been moved.

However, it's very seldom that someone actually witnesses the transportation. In poltergeist cases, the surroundings are affected in a sudden, dramatic, and often volatile way. It's as if they're struck by some violent eruption of energy that makes a raw and unpredictable impact on the environment. Though mysterious sounds, and the sense of a physical touch, can certainly be experienced as well, the influence is usually most notable on physical objects.

A thirty-year-old woman, Deborah, had been suffering from poltergeist activity for nearly two years. She had always assumed the occurrences were caused by a disruptive entity. In fact, she believed the spirit was terrorizing her individually, since the activity was most prominent in her presence. Not only did Deborah fear what this invisible force might be capable of doing, but she found the activity embarrassing, especially since it "followed" her. Deborah's social life had gone down the drain completely. She was afraid that once people noticed this happening around her, they would think she was possessed, or that she was a practitioner of witchcraft. In either case, it would demand a strange explanation from her, and that was an issue that made her extremely uncomfortable.

After investigating her home for several hours, my colleagues and I were quickly able to determine that paranormal activity was, in fact, happening there. We picked up massive fluctuations of electromagnetic and infrared energy, and noted objects that seemed to have moved on several occasions. Some photographs showed strange "washed out" areas around Deborah. At the end of the evening, a fellow researcher and I sat on a couch facing Deborah, who stood in front of us. Behind her, on the wall, was a serene painting. On either side of the picture was a decorative, wooden dove, each hung on the wall by a nail. The desperate woman was pleased to hear we'd documented some enigmatic occurrences in her home. Next, her attention turned completely to how we might end this activity. I was open and honest with her, telling her there was no guaranteed way of stopping the phenomena. As soon as the reality and impact of my words settled with her, I watched a gloom drop about her face and a new hardness shine in her eyes. And then, it happened.

We were looking right at Deborah. On the wall behind her, there was a burst of motion. One of the decorative doves launched off the wall in an explosion of energy. It soared several feet, flying in a great arc, then crashed to the floor, pieces blasting everywhere. When it happened, a kind of palpable shock wave—a stiff breeze of indescribable energy—hit us in the face. It was like the room had shaken, and I sat stunned, in true awe. At that point, Deborah dropped her head in the bleakest of ways. With a weak and defeated stillness about her, she squatted down and began slowly gathering up the fragments. She mumbled something like, "That happens all the time."

What happened when the wooden dove came off that wall? Was it thrown off the wall by an entity who didn't like a discussion about his removal? Or was it the product of a telekinetic burst by Deborah? When she realized there was not some simple, clean solution to her problem, was the thought so disconcerting that her stress instigated a telekinetic expenditure? Though Deborah said she'd never consciously produced a telekinetic effect, she did feel she had some psychic ability. This was especially with regard to telepathic experiences.

Though it is possible that some entity was responsible for these events, we never observed or documented any direct evidence for such a being. Time after time, the activity affected the physical surroundings, and whenever something significant occurred, Deborah was present. You must diagnose a situation based on the symptoms. It seemed undeniable that we were smack in the middle of a poltergeist case. The activity was clearly dependent on the presence of the agent. You may wonder why not *all* of the occurrences took place when she was around. Perhaps all the *genuine* paranormal activity did. However, people do make mistakes from time to time, believing they've witnessed a supernatural event when they've really just experienced an optical illusion or something more mundane. But, in a place known to be haunted, people tend to automatically blame everything on the ghosts. If you're in a haunted house and a mouse runs across the floor, creating a vague sense of motion accompanied by a noise, it's easy to say it was a ghostly manifestation. It would be convenient to assume that's what you experienced. Perhaps events as ordinary as that were interpreted as paranormal when Deborah was not around.

To this day, Deborah still experiences the activity from time to time. She's one of those rare people who may be surrounded by these incidents throughout her whole life. On several occasions, I've asked her to participate in telekinesis experiments. However, she refuses. She seems to be sincerely fearful of finding that she might be capable of producing the effects. It seems, in her mind, it makes her closer to a sorcerer, something she believes is evil, something that defies her Christian religion.

Poltergeist activity can be some of the most spectacular phenomena in the world of paranormal research. It's rare to witness physical effects like those in a ghost movie, but that's just what poltergeists can provide. Whether it is the product of an entity that feeds from the individual, or that person's own psychic ability, it is a powerful affair. Humans possess tremendous energy potential. When that potential is effectively tapped, it can create remarkable and drastic changes in the environment.

There is one more thing you should keep in mind when studying this kind of activity. Whatever creates the poltergeist phenomenon, it is, in at least some way, dependent on utilizing human energy. The mechanism by which this occurs is currently unknown. However, the process of drawing energy, regardless of exactly how it works, seems to affect the agent's mind as well as his or her body. An agent can be a volatile and fickle individual. He can fluctuate between being extremely courteous and kind to being rude and inconsiderate. An agent's mind can certainly be clouded or misguided by the activity. When associating with the person, be cautious. In some cases, you may have to humor him to quell a spontaneous violent tendency.

All in all, it is usually difficult to study poltergeist activity systematically because of its brevity and the stress it imposes on the agent. Therefore, investigators who do have the fortune of witnessing it should make the most of this rare and spectacular phenomenon. A better understanding of these cases should lead to a deeper understanding of the human psyche and, perhaps most importantly, its complex relationship with our physical surroundings.

Poltergeist activity:
1. Is dependent upon the presence of a specific individual or individuals.
2. Usually makes the biggest impact on physical objects.
3. Is usually temporary.

NATURALS

Earlier in the book, I touched upon the difference between ghostly phenomena and what *appear* to be ghostly phenomena. Once again, the point can be illustrated with a common magnet. If in ancient times a person placed a piece of iron near a magnet, he witnessed a seemingly mystical effect. Some invisible force would grab hold of the iron and pull it through the air to slam tight against the loadstone. The experience was sudden, powerful, and repeatable. People had no way of making sense of this occurrence; they could not clearly compare it to any other aspect of their lives. Because of this, magnetite was understandably considered a magical substance with supernatural powers. However, science was eventually able to explain this ghostly effect in terms that had nothing to do with ghosts at all. We would call this a NATURAL: a rare phenomenon that appears ghostly but in fact is created by some scientifically unknown property of the present nature. Note the word *present.* Under our loose definition, ghostly activity is the paranormal remnant of something apart from its original manifestation, usually meaning "from the past." A natural is completely of its time. It simply happens to mimic activity that appears ghostly to casual human observation.

Brown Mountain is a long, low-lying ridge in the Pisgah National Forest, on the border of Burke and Caldwell counties in western North Carolina. Over the past century, it has become internationally famous for its "ghost lights." According to local legend, the Cherokee and Catawba Indians waged a vicious battle on the ridge, sometime around the year 1200. It was said that the warriors ceremoniously marched into battle, torches blazing. When the fighting was over, the mourning women ventured onto the ridge at night, searching for their slain loved ones, also by torchlight. Soon after the event, the lights began appearing on the mountain. It has always been a popular notion that the eerie glows on Brown Mountain are caused by the wandering spirits of the Indians, their torches still burning.

The ridge is a rugged and treacherous place to venture. Parts of it are marked by dangerous, rocky trails. They can be navigated only on foot, horseback, or all-terrain vehicles. It's also a black bear reserve, and deadly snakes, like copperheads, make snug homes between the granite slabs. Because it's so inconvenient to reach and explore, the lights are usually seen from overlooks several miles away. At that distance, they can still be seen brightly, but descriptions of them vary.

The illuminations are generally "balls of light" that can be virtually any color. However, they're most often white, orange, yellow, or red. Their appearance is spontaneous and unpredictable. You might watch the mountain for weeks and not see one. Then, sensationally, they appear. You could see one light that sits on the ridge, halfway down, for a minute. It might flare up for a few seconds, then dwindle for a few, then flare up again, and so on. When doing this, they're most often red on the mountain, turning white when they flare most brightly. Or, you might see some of the strangest activity of all: The light might begin to move—dance around a bit . . .

then split into three or four smaller lights, each one appearing to sort of orbit around the others. Next, the lights could line up and move across the ridge, just like souls marching with torches. This phantasmal line will meander over the top of the ridge and vanish, or sometimes simply reach a point where it dwindles and becomes a vague, dispersing light.

The Brown Mountain Lights have baffled scientists. They've been investigated at least three times by the United States government; twice by the Geological Survey and once by the Weather Service. Even the Smithsonian Institution, in Washington, D.C., sent a group of researchers. Starting in the late 1970s, ORION (the Oak Ridge Isochronous Observation Network), a team of scientists from the Oak Ridge National Laboratory, spent a decade camping on the mountain and conducting a barrage of experiments. Researchers tested the possibility of natural gas, mirages, plasmas, and other usual suspects. However, in no case was a provable explanation found. For many, this has enhanced the possibility of extraterrestrial activity, ghostly manifestations, or some other esoteric phenomenon.

The phenomenon also inspired lots of creative minds. They were the basis of the hit bluegrass song "Brown Mountain Light," which debuted in the 1960s. They've been featured in numerous works of fiction and nonfiction, such as Andy Anderson's novel *Kill One, Kill Two*, and were even the basis of a 1999 episode of *The X-Files* television series. Despite all the interest, the enigma remained.

The Brown Mountain Lights were first journalistically documented in 1912. Even though, over so many years, such a great number of people had seen them, the lights were virtually impossible to capture on motion picture film or video. Though they are bright to the naked eye, they are still miles away, against a dim horizon. The first known video footage of the phenomenon was captured in the fall of 2000. I'm proud to say, it was obtained by L.E.M.U.R.

During a series of L.E.M.U.R. expeditions that fall, we witnessed the lights in full force. On most occasions, the team's vice president and imaging specialist, Brian Irish, wielded his infrared night-vision digital video camera. In the footage, not only were the lights visible, but the ridge itself could also be seen, allowing us to study the specific places on the mountain where the lights appeared. Our investigation of Brown Mountain is still in progress. What do we think they are?

Currently, there is absolutely no proof for any explanation of the Brown Mountain Lights. Being ghost researchers, most people expect us to say we think they're ghosts. After all, they appear consistent with the ghost stories. However, though we certainly don't feel we have the explanation, we're tending to think there's no reason to jump to a ghostly conclusion.

Brown Mountain is composed of cranberry granite and displays no extraordinary quality. However, it is almost completely encircled by thrust faults. These are places where one slab of earth slides over on top of another. They can grind back and forth, causing a good deal of stress. The area contains a lot of quartz. Whenever you apply pressure to any rock or crystal, it creates electricity. In fact, you can smash a sugar cube with a hammer and see a flash of blue energy. This is especially the case with quartz, though. You may have seen or used a cigarette lighter that ignites the butane with an electrical spark. This is created by squeezing a piece of quartz. The effect is called "piezoelectricity."

It is possible the faults create electricity that influences the area. The ground may actually conduct these charges, or they might simply manifest in bursts that create strong electromagnetic fields in the area. It's also possible that static-electrical energy on the mountain combines with the electromagnetic environment, creating a rare form of stable plasma, otherwise known as ball lightning. Scientists still do not understand exactly how ball lightning is created. However, it is clearly an electrical manifestation.

It seems the Brown Mountain Lights are objective balls of glowing energy. They appear inexplicably, then vanish just the same. And those who are near them say they can interact with your body. This activity is certainly "ghostly," but can we say this describes a true ghost? Perhaps it does, but it might also describe an electrical phenomenon, sensitive and reactant to the electrical fields of the human body. So, what should we conclude?

We should always assume as little as possible when defining facts. The simplest explanation usually ends up being the correct one. You want to rule out all conventional phenomena before resorting to ghostly explanations. The Brown Mountain Lights could be the product of spirits, or they could be a natural phenomenon. But which is more likely?

In terms of evidence, we have pictures and footage of strange lights moving around a mountain. We have no documentation of them taking on conscious interactions, despite unconfirmed stories. We can't even prove whether or not the Native American battle took place. Where does that leave us?

Whatever they are, there is no reason to jump to a supernatural conclusion. *That* conclusion should always be saved as a last resort. Therefore, we end up with what is probably a nice example of a "natural"—a phenomenon that appears consistent with ghostly activity but is in fact an unfamiliar manifestation of nature. This kind of category shows just how fine and efficient a paranormal investigator's sense of judgment must be.

Naturals are of great importance. They define "ghostly

activity" that is, in fact, not the product of a ghost. But they are grouped under "ghostly activity" because, at face value, they seem to be. As an investigator, your job is to explore new territories. If you explore phenomena that you already know are the product of a ghost, then apparently someone has beaten you to the punch. If you are a true virgin researcher, you will witness things that perhaps no one has ever seen before. It might fall on your shoulders to set a precedent, and determine whether or not a thing is a ghost. In that situation, you must carefully consider the evidence before drawing a conclusion. Your reputation as an analyst is at stake.

Many mainstream sciences laugh at the idea of spiritual phenomena. This is because mankind has cried wolf too many times, calling something spiritual when it was not. As we all know, a caveman might describe an airplane or a television as supernatural. The only way we can change this attitude is by applying the deepest level of consideration to what we identify as a ghost. Before you determine the activity meets that definition, be sure to examine every other possibility. You might ask: How can I tell the difference between a ghost—something I don't fully understand—and an unknown natural property, something else I don't understand? The key to answering this question is recognizing how natural properties and laws tend to work. This takes time.

Imagine if you were the first person to notice that when you rub a piece of glass on fur, it will attract small objects, like feathers and strings, via static electricity. The first thing you would conclude is that it was caused by rubbing the glass. However, you would notice that it doesn't happen every time. After experimenting and observing enough, you should find that humidity makes the difference. Then, you could experiment with how different kinds of charges can be created using different things. Ultimately, you should find patterns—consistent connections between what you do and what occurs. Science develops in this way, testing out unknown variables and recording the "ingredients" when a desired effect is, or is not, achieved.

When observing an unknown phenomenon, be sure to watch for patterns of activity and record what happens. You might eventually conclude you've been watching some rare process of nature, but not necessarily an activity that fits our definition of a ghost. Ability in this area can separate a true scientist from a pseudoscientist.

A natural is:

1. A rare phenomenon that appears ghostly, but in fact is created by some scientifically unknown property of the present nature.

A SUMMARY OF GHOSTS

When the average Joe thinks of a ghost, he simply envisions the spirit of a dead person. This is because that's *usually* what a ghost seems to be—an entity. However, as you've seen, that is still just one of several possibilities. The casual layperson may never need to know anything more about ghosts, but a paranormal investigator should be aware of all known possibilities, however rare. Throughout the decades, there has been a tendency to break up ghostly activity into three categories: entities, imprints, and poltergeists. By updating these divisions, and adding two more, we are staying current with the new information we're gaining, in large part due to newer technology.

As you have also seen, this singular idea of a ghost has vast implications. We've discussed psychic phenomena, philosophical questions like the mind-body dilemma, theoretical physics and space/time, the nature of matter and energy, and the infinite possibilities of future discoveries. It's easy to see why a good paranormal researcher must be an intelligent, knowledgeable person with keen awareness and the ability to scientifically analyze information in a realistic way.

We shall not, for an instant, pretend that the information presented, or the way in which it was presented, is absolute gospel. You must never forget that we are studying a mystery. That means all the answers are not known. Therefore, unknown facts *must* exist that would have a definite effect on how we categorize activity and define its physical nature.

Most of the general public's knowledge of ghosts has been passed on in the form of entertainment. Campfire ghost stories, horror novels, and scary movies have provided the foundation. Storytellers want their tales to make a memorable impact on audiences. To accomplish this, they've always focused on a simple concept: dead people can come back. This makes for great storytelling because it creates a strong impression. It would be too confusing to expect the general public to understand the difference between entities, imprints, warps, poltergeists, and naturals. In stories, it's nice and clean to focus on one concept. However, as in so many instances, real life is far more complex and confusing than we like to visualize.

Ghost stories are also constructed to give you a surprise ending. That's the ironic moment when suddenly all the details fall into place, and a chill runs down your spine. It's always a fun moment. However, that moment rarely comes in real investigations. Usually, there isn't a time when everything falls magically into place. Though you may learn a lot, also expect to leave with new questions and, sometimes, an unsatisfied feeling. That's the nature of a true mystery.

When you conduct your own investigations, and you're trying to decide exactly what kind of activity you're dealing with, don't be discouraged if you find the task more difficult than expected. Even though we have separated the phenomena into five categories, always keep in mind that one haunted location may exhibit more than one type. For example, it's not that uncommon to discover a place where entities and imprints coexist. Perhaps someone was murdered in a house: An imprint of the murder may still be observed, and the conscious entity of the victim might remain in the home as well. A warp location can display manifestations of every category. Labeling ghostly activity can be somewhat confusing because it represents our current level of understanding it. Though we have developed a great deal over the past few decades, our understanding is still in its infancy. But that's what's so exciting about it.

As you research ghosts in a systematic way, you'll soon find out just how strange some of the activity can be. You're bound to quickly encounter situations more outlandish than anything mentioned in this book. But that's truly what makes this kind of research so much fun and interesting. Whenever I go to a haunted location, I really have no idea what's going to happen. After you go to enough places, you'll stop even trying to anticipate what you'll find. Here, in the twenty-first century, humans are used to immediately recognizing and understanding almost everything we see. Therefore, when we see something we *don't* immediately recognize, it fills us with a primitive rush of wonder, the kind our ancient ancestors must have experienced much more frequently. What did a caveman think upon seeing fire for the first time? You may think you've evolved past that emotion, but it's there, I guarantee you. Sooner or later, you will feel it.

This part of the book has given you a general understanding of the theories regarding ghostly activity. They provide a starting point from which your understanding can grow and develop. But, as usual, things work one way on paper and another way in reality. This can especially be the case when it comes to something like the paranormal. And so, since you are now familiar with the subject matter, we'll move into the area of practical applications. You will now learn how to actually hunt ghosts.

PART TWO:

GHOST HUNTING

WHY HUNT GHOSTS?

Now that you have a basic understanding of the theories behind ghostly activity, it's time to use them in the field. But first, we will directly address the question of why one should want to investigate the spectral. The implications of humans' surviving physical death ring most strongly. Nineteenth-century historian H. T. Buckle said: "If immortality be untrue, it matters little whether anything else be true or not." The idea of surviving physical death is synonymous with immortality. It is a desire for immortality that has nourished most of the world's religions. Regardless of one's views on the existence of an afterlife, those views affect how one lives this physical life. In this sense, even if an afterlife does not exist, the mere possibility that it *could* exist has drastically shaped mankind. Our civilization is based upon laws; those laws are usually based on morals; those morals are usually based on religions; and religions are usually inspired by the idea of an afterlife.

For thousands of years, the concept of surviving death has been nearly impossible to study. But now, as we enter the twenty-first century, our technology and understanding of the universe is making it possible to explore the subtle energies associated with life. We are still far from a complete explanation, but we are moving closer each day. Ghostly activity is currently the most efficient link to scientific study of the concept of an afterlife. If science is able to unequivocally prove the existence of spiritual phenomena, it will revolutionize the world.

For instance, if we are able to completely understand how imprints are made, the entire past might be at our fingertips. As parapsychologist Loyd Auerbach pointed out in the February 2000 issue of *Fate* magazine:

> *If locations (and objects) actually do somehow record information through time, in effect being historical recording devices, and somehow that information can be retrieved, either through human perceptions or some new technology, think of the applications! History can be accessed at any location. Therefore, the world becomes a recording device. People could access past events for education or entertainment.*

Imagine a day when you can take a special pair of goggles and headphones to any location and, by tuning through various "frequencies," watch any moment in that location's past. It would literally be a kind of audio/visual time travel. This is truly the substance of thrilling science fiction. Perhaps an intense event can create an impression some humans can sometimes see. But what if all activity, however mundane, creates an impression, as well—an impression so distant and weak that powerful new technology is necessary to recall it. We may someday rewrite history, given an ability to see it as it actually occurred. It might also change the way we conduct ourselves. What if, after you sell your house, the new owners could view everything you ever did on the property? Goodness knows what a motel room would yield.

The success of our civilization depends largely on our understanding of the relationship between humans and their environment. This can be clearly illustrated by sanitation. For thousands of years, humans did not realize how disease was enhanced and spread by improper waste management. In 1348 England, residents would actually toss their refuse into the streets. Layers of rotting garbage, several feet thick, lined the city. This is one of the major reasons why plagues like the Black Death killed so many people. Poltergeist activity addresses another aspect of humans' relationship with the environment. Regardless of the exact nature of the association, studying this phenomenon can only deepen our ability to further improve our society.

Warps play at the fringes of theoretical science. They make us ask questions that irritate the uncomfortable valley where science and philosophy merge. Before Einstein came along, much of what is now considered science was then considered metaphysical or at least philosophical. Topics like time travel and manipulating this substance, space/time, had virtually no basis in hard-core facts and evidence. In fact, to most, they seemed too abstract to think about in a standardized way. We're ultimately talking about understanding the actual substance of reality—matter and energy—and the process by which it functions. As time passes, we find more and more reasons to believe that reality is a flexible and inconsistent thing. Therefore, it holds many capabilities beyond the ordinary human experience. Warps may be places where reality behaves in a more fluid way. In fact, these might even be areas where it's easier for mankind to manipulate reality, given the proper knowledge and tools. We are still far from understanding how reality is formed. If it does have seams, these may be the places we experience as warps.

Naturals are a combination of nature's most mysterious puzzles and human beings' infinite ability to project their own ideas onto that blank slate. We have places where physical activity is still misunderstood by mainstream science, and they represent the purest of wonders. Reality is a combination of what we can prove to exist and how we choose to see it. Even though subjective reality is not as scientifically valid as objective reality, it's *still* a form of reality. If two people see a strange light in the sky, then agree neither can identify it, what comes next? At that point, perhaps you would view it as a spaceship with aliens, or a secret device the government is testing. To each person, his own view may seem the more likely. However, who is more correct? Both observers share the objective evidence— 50 percent of the equation—since they saw the same thing. In this case, the other half of the equation is the subjective evidence. Until further objective evidence can be gained, the two people are left with something that is only half real. The other half is a muddy swirl of conjectures. Naturals seem half real in the same way. They are documented phenomena, but ones that cannot be completely explained. Whenever there is an enduring mystery, it holds something new to learn.

But, despite the grand causes of ghost research, there are many small, simple, and personal reasons to conduct such work. Some people who witness the paranormal regularly want to confirm their sanity. If someone who does not believe in ghosts sees one, this person has to make a decision: Do I now believe ghosts are real? Or am I insane? Either way, it can be a big decision. I am frequently contacted by owners of haunted houses who don't want to accept the activity, yet want me to investigate to see what can be confirmed. If I am able to document ghosts, the owner is usually relieved.

Others want to rid their homes of unwanted spiritual presences. We'll discuss this subject more later. But you must realize that the roles of ghost hunter and "ghost buster" or exorcist are not the same. By the same token, people understandably want to communicate with a departed soul. In this case, I must affirm that a scientific ghost hunter is not a medium, or one who channels spirits. The subject of communication with spirits will be addressed later as well.

Some businesses view haunting activity as an added attraction and want to prove it exists in order to increase profits. This is especially the case in old hotels, inns, and bed-and-breakfasts. Through the years, so many guests pass through these locations that deaths and tragedies inevitably occur from time to time. For a while, after such instances take place, it's usually considered taboo to discuss the sensitive subjects. However, if the occurrence gives rise to a ghost, the memory of the incident is kept alive far into the future, long after those directly involved in the original incident have died or moved on. If benevolent, the spirit eventually becomes an endearing part of the location's culture. As long as the activity is genuine, it's no different from publicizing the scenery, the accommodations, or any other asset.

Lots of ghost hunters do it simply for the thrill of the chase—much like a hunter of wild game. There's nothing wrong with this, as long as they treat the sport respectfully. A lot of people become involved for this reason, but last a very short period of time. That's because ghost hunting requires patience. One might tediously investigate hundreds of places for years without ever seeing an apparition with the naked eyes. Many do not realize just how rare such an experience can be. However, that's really the key to the entire field: Value comes with rarity, and there is enormous value in witnessing a phenomenon that seemingly defies the laws of physics. When these instances occur, they are well worth the amount of time and effort invested in researching them.

Paranormal research is not as sensational as movies, television, and fictional writings would have you believe. Usually, for each significant event recorded, hundreds or thousands of hours are invested. Most investigations are somewhat boring—quietly observing vacant areas and equipment readings. You may spend days in a location and see nothing at all; or you might walk in the door and have an encounter in thirty seconds. It's spontaneous and fairly unpredictable—but *that's why it's special.* If you want to see ghosts guaranteed, buy a ticket to Orlando and visit the funhouse. But if you want to experience legitimate activity in the real world, you must be a realistic person. Those who want to conduct paranormal research for excitement must first pay their dues in diligence and patience. In most cases, only the most devoted make the cut.

Even though it is uncommon to see ghosts with the naked eye, it is far more common to capture photographs of them. To succeed in doing so, one must use instruments to unveil the spiritual world hidden from our senses, then wield a camera appropriately. A ghost researcher's trophy is usually a good photograph. At this point in time, our understanding of spirits is so limited that we're still at the stage of trying to capture as much visual information as possible, especially in combination with objective energy readings. In the coming chapters, you'll be shown the most effective techniques to do so.

There are lots of reasons to hunt ghosts. Generally speaking, *any* new knowledge we obtain about *any* facet of the universe improves our collective understanding of existence. The better we understand life, the higher our chances of enjoying it most, or maximizing our potential to augment it. The ultimate goal of all science is to improve mankind's experience via greater understanding of the world. As your reputation as a ghost hunter grows, you'll encounter people with new and unusual motivations for spiritual research. Always remember: Whatever you choose to investigate, your intention should be to benefit life and the collective human experience. Never venture into the spectral realm with ill intentions. As in all aspects of life, your actions will yield reactions.

FINDING GHOSTS

Finding where ghosts hang out is usually easy. Virtually any location can prove to be haunted. Ghost stories are widely passed by word of mouth. Of course, not all ghost stories are true. Creepy-looking places, like decrepit, old houses or cemeteries, are often assumed to be haunted due to the stereotypes popular culture has given us. Lots of ghost stories are invented for pure entertainment value—having a good yarn to spin around the campfire. But, in many cases, ghost stories, though embellished, do have a basis in fact. You're liable to find that locations rumored to be haunted do indeed demonstrate unusual activity. But keep in mind that any place, no matter how modern, can be a stomping ground for spirits. Just because a new structure is built, that does not mean the land upon which it is built could not have an intense past. In the United States alone, so many people, from Native Americans and European settlers to fallen Civil War soldiers, have died across the land that one can never tell where energies may be housed.

In the region where I live, there is a town called Canton. It is the headquarters for one of the world's largest paper manufacturers. The livelihood of the entire town is dependent upon the enormous mill, and over the years, the company has been criticized for their handling of pollutants. Great smoke-stacks soar above the buildings, pumping thick, dark clouds into the sky. A sickening, putrid odor rolls like fog, pouring into the mountainous valleys, hanging and lingering like a curse. As one drives down the nearby interstate, it becomes obvious when the town draws near. The aroma seeps into the car, and most hold their breath, pressing the accelerator a little harder to leave the area behind.

With a dreary description like that, it's difficult to understand how so many live long, pleasant, peaceful lives in Canton. The hills around the factory are rowed with cozy cottages and quiet homes. It is a scenic area, yet so tainted by the smell. If you ask residents how they tolerate the odor, they will smile and proclaim, "I don't even smell it!" This makes a powerful statement about the mind. When we don't want to be conscious of something we're subjected to, the brain will eventually filter it out. It's a subconscious defense mechanism. The same thing occurs when one lives next to a busy highway: eventually, the annoying sounds of the passing automobiles are tuned out. Similarly, it is possible that we tune out ghostly things occurring around us each day. Do we perhaps catch a glimpse of the spectral more often than we think, but usually choose to ignore it as a fantasy or an optical illusion?

Though most people associate ghosts exclusively with graveyards and melancholy residences, there's really no basis for it. In many cases, conscious spirits choose a sociable environment, just like the living. For this reason, restaurants, hotels, and ballrooms are often visited by phantoms. If you were a ghost, what places would you frequent? The answer to that question may provide good leads.

Of course, those spooky old houses and graveyards frequently display activity as well. It is difficult to understand why a conscious entity would frequent a dreary place. It's possible that such a being's options are restricted. Maybe ghosts can't roam wherever they please, due to conditions we do not understand. We can understand why an imprint would remain in the same place. But how about an entity? Perhaps all entities can travel as they choose. However, maybe they can material- ize in some places more easily in others. When you live in a particular location for years, you saturate that place with your energy. It becomes your *home*. Upon returning in a spiritual form, it may be easier for you to manifest in your home. Your energy in life might prepare your access in death. This is an area that deserves much research. However, even though investigat- ing places like cemeteries may yield results, you should remember some ethical guidelines about researching them.

Everyone loves the idea of ghosts haunting graveyards at night. Indeed, those who venture onto such sacred grounds at evening often do find activity. However, lots of ghost researchers disdain visiting these locations after dark. You must remember the basic purpose for cemeteries: to provide eternal rest for fallen loved ones. Whether or not "rest" is achieved in any practical way, it certainly takes place in a sym- bolic one. It is generally considered disrespectful to enter cemeteries at night. Aside from that, it is often considered trespassing. On those occasions when I have done this, it was always prearranged with the caretaker. Even then, I was once surprised when several police cars sped into the place, lights flashing, and officers ordered me and my colleagues to lie on the ground. A neighbor, unaware of my arrangement with the caretaker, had called the cops upon seeing a group in the graveyard at night. Unfortunately, so many tombstones are vandalized, and graves desecrated, that most are paranoid about seeing people on sacred ground in the evening. Obviously, you should never trespass, regardless of the loca- tion. Always be respectful of the law and the property owners.

If you hear that a place is haunted, say a house, don't be too shy to call the owners, or write them a letter, to explain who you are and why you'd like to investigate the place. Of course, you must be prepared for any response. Some people will think you're a weirdo for simply asking, while others are actually ashamed of their ghosts. This is especially the case with extremely religious people. Unfortunately, some religions stress that ghostly activity is inherently evil and cannot be the product of God or His holy design. Those types of individuals can go to great lengths to prevent spreading news of their hauntings. They are generally afraid their peers will consider them loony at best, and practitioners of witchcraft at worst. When you encounter these sorts, it's best to simply apologize for disturbing them, and carry your interests elsewhere. There are plenty of active places, so there's no use wasting time at an inaccessible location.

On the other hand, there are just as many property owners who will gladly volunteer information about their hauntings. These people can be interested for a number of reasons. They might share a fascination for afterlife research, or simply view a resident ghost as a nice conversation piece, something to add a little personality to the place. Many want to know more about the history of their property, and believe that learning about their spirits can help give them details otherwise unavailable. Even more people are simply curious. These are the types of people most helpful to a ghost investigator. Remember, just like skiing requires snow, ghost hunting requires an active location—and locations have owners. You must make them feel comfortable with your intentions, and have infinite respect for their generosity.

If you're looking for ghosts, ask around your community to find haunted places. Once word gets out that you're looking, folks will probably start contacting you. Nine times out of ten, when conversing with strangers, once I mention my field of research, someone inevitably brings up a haunted location. Whether they believe in ghosts or not, everyone hears memorable stories from time to time. They are an indelible part of our culture.

Of course, the media love to publicize haunted places around Halloween. Keep your eye on newspapers and magazines in October. You're bound to find some great locations. Though the activity in such places is often exaggerated by the media, they are still valuable areas to research. You can gain credibility by visiting well-known haunts. The general public sees them as way points for a ghost hunter, and whether or not the location is genuinely active, your experience there gives you weight when comparing one area's activity to another.

You can hunt ghosts at any time of the day and year. However, the best times seem to be the cold, dry months of winter and fall. At many North American locations, this is when static electricity is most active. It is also best to search for ghosts after dark. There are several reasons for this. For one thing, the illumination of apparitions will be more pronounced. As I covered earlier in the book, materializations often appear to be electrical coronas, and these can be faint. It is especially advisable to allow your eyes to adjust to the dark, enlarging your pupils. This greatly increases your chances of clearly seeing a weak illumination.

It seems the peak time for spectral encounters is from midnight to around four in the morning. These hours are the most peaceful and unobtrusive since most people are asleep and electrical devices (which might interfere with or disrupt activity) are turned off. There's a sense of calm about this time span, and that's always good for obtaining uncontaminated results. But nighttime is also better for a more cosmically significant reason.

As you know, the earth is surrounded by a magnetic field. This field is called the "magnetosphere." It emerges from the poles, and bows around the planet, far into space, shaped like the field from a traditional loadstone magnet. It completely envelops earth and plays a vital role in our survival. The sun is the largest nuclear reaction in the solar system. It is constantly blasting earth with devastating radiation (Illus. 9). We would be killed by this energy if our planet's atmosphere were not able to deflect and absorb it. The magnetosphere is our first and most powerful line of defense. It shields our delicate planet from the sun's massive discharge. Imagine the field of the earth three-dimensionally: Since it emerges from the poles, the field is shaped like a funnel in those areas. Near the poles, the field is therefore thinner (where it dips down), and this allows more of the sun's radiation to bleed through. That's why, near the poles, the Northern and Southern Lights, known respectively as the "Aurora Borealis" and the

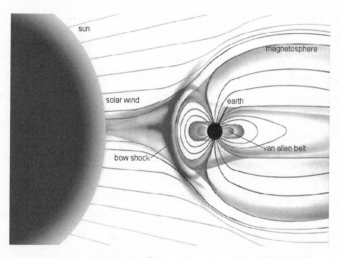

9. The magnetosphere calms at night, possibly enhancing perception of the ghostly. *Courtesy Robert McGhee*

"Aurora Australis," are visible. They are caused by the sun's radiation exciting particles in the atmosphere, similar to how electrons passing through a neon tube cause the gas to glow.

Even though the magnetosphere defies the sun's excessive radiation, it is still affected by it. As the planet's field naturally emerges from the poles, its lines of force should extend into space parallel to one another. However, when the sun's rays hit the field, they compress it, mashing it down closer to the planet and distorting its shape. Therefore, on the side of the earth facing the sun, the field is aggravated and disrupted. The opposite side of the planet, the nighttime side, remains unaffected. That side of the magnetosphere is not being compressed by the sun, therefore it extends farther into space, opening up the fields to create a calm energy environment. When the field expands, it lifts the ionosphere, off of which electromagnetic waves reflect. At night, you can pick up radio stations that are hundreds or thousands of miles away. This is because their signals reflect from the heightened ionosphere at a greater angle, reaching farther, and through a calmer, less disrupted, energy setting.

Obviously, a great deal of ghostly activity is detected by measuring subtle energies. You can easily imagine how such energies are affected by the sun's radiation. These delicate manifestations can be overwhelmed by solar rays. Their fine frequencies can become lost in the blaze of energy. However, at night, when the electromagnetic environment is calm, it is obviously easier for us to find and follow spectral manifestations. It should also be easier for spirits to materialize. Just as radio waves are heightened at night, ghostly activity may increase in a similar fashion.

The amount of solar radiation bombarding the earth varies. Energy blazes off the sun inconsistently. The radiation forms enormous bands—loops of fiery plasma—that extend from the sun and sear deep into space. When these bands sometimes break, they release a charge of radiation that hurtles into the magnetosphere. These are simply called "solar flares." A low-level flare is called C Class, a medium, M Class, and a high burst, an X Class. Powerful X Class flares can seriously disrupt, or destroy, earth's communications and satellite technology. You can monitor the type of solar activity the planet is experiencing via several web sites, including my own. A hot topic of research for paranormal investigators is the specific relationship between these solar flares and unexplainable activity. High solar turmoil should prove an obstacle to some manifestations—just like ordinary solar activity seems to do during the day. On the other hand, it may serve to enhance another type of phenomenon, like a warp location. During your research, you should try to document the solar conditions whenever possible, comparing them to your findings in search of correlations.

Similarly, some investigators believe the phase of the moon may affect paranormal occurrences. Clearly, the moon has an effect on our planet, such as the rising of the oceans' tides. It's often reported that full moons increase the crime rate and influence the body's fluids—making surgery dangerous due to problems regarding blood flow. However, serious studies of these reports have never proven a consistent correlation between the moon and effects on individuals. But, considering the moon's impact on tides, it may also influence the degree to which the spiritual world becomes active, or at least accessible. For now, we can't say for certain; there seems to be no clear evidence either way. Nonetheless, it is important to document the moon phase, along with all other environmental information, when conducting research. Sooner or later, definite correlations may arise.

Even though we don't yet understand the exact relationship between the earth, sun, moon, and ghosts, you'll generally have your best research results when the cloak of darkness falls. Keep this in mind when scheduling investigations. Night owls make the best researchers. Of course, darkness also lends itself to fertile imaginations. Be sure you don't let your fantasies run wild.

WHAT TO LOOK FOR

There is invisible life teeming all around you. Not only is it unseen, but you can't feel it or hear it. In fact, you might never know it is there unless you have a microscope. This simple tool allows us to peer into an entire realm of existence unknown to man before 1590, when the microscope was invented. Of course, that device could not have existed without the development of the lens in the 1200s. As our technology increases, so does our awareness of more life forms around us.

A ghost may be standing right next to you, but you might not know. Though they are present, specters are rarely seen or heard with naked human senses. This seems to be because of their dependency on environmental conditions to materialize. However, even if you cannot always perceive them with your bare senses, you can still monitor, access, and photograph them using the proper detection equipment. It is by employing such means that ghost hunters acquire most of their results.

Ghosts are apparently composed of a substance that occupies a frequency different from physical matter. They might be comparable to radio waves, for example. At any given moment, man-made radio waves usually surround us, and in fact, permeate us. However, they are invisible and silent; we also can't reach out and feel them. One might never know they were around without the assistance of a radio. The radio is a tool made for sensing and interpreting these waves. A radio allows you to tap in to that invisible realm. In the same way, if you know what kinds of energies to look for, and you have the proper tools, you can detect phantoms even if they are not apparent to your naked senses.

Most ghostly activity is accompanied by erratic, fluctuating fields of electromagnetic energy. Therefore, we use devices that detect and measure such energy to hunt them. Human eyes cannot usually perceive these fields of energy. For a ghost to visually materialize, it is often dependent upon electrostatic charges in the air. Even if the electrical environment is not suitable for materialization, we can still detect ghosts using the proper tools. Again, it's sort of like a magnet: If iron filings are available, you can "see" the magnetic lines. But even if they are not available, you can detect magnetic lines by holding a compass near them. In the same way, the conditions to "see" a ghost may not be right, but you can still detect them.

Regardless of the type of ghost you're dealing with—be it an entity, imprint, etc.—you use the same basic techniques to research them. With the exception of those unpredictable warp manifestations, all ghosts produce the same electromagnetic and electrostatic influences. This means that the general way in which you gather objective evidence does not vary. In all ghost investigations, the same scientific tools apply. Determining what kind of ghost you're dealing with is based on your ability to document the unique characteristics of the activity.

Areas of a location where most of the activity is concentrated are called "hot spots." You want to try to find these places by comparing data taken from various sections of the locale. Some rooms in a haunted house may yield little or no anomalous energy, while others produce extraordinary amounts. You'll frequently find that areas where ghosts have appeared regularly correspond with constant pools of excessive electromagnetic energy. While many hot spots demonstrate consistent energy masses, others may not always be active. In fact, they might become active only during a certain time of day, or under the appropriate weather conditions.

A place may be a hot spot for any number of reasons. It might be the specific space where a significant event took place, as with an imprint. It could simply be an entity's favorite site. In many cases, it seems they might be areas where ghosts can use the excess energy for materialization. When investigating a haunt, you will often find all of the prominent activity centralized around one grand hot spot.

You should also note that a lot of spiritual activity takes place around mirrors—particularly in a room where two mirrors are facing each other. This may be because mirrors reflect electromagnetic energy. It's possible that, when two mirrors face, they create a highly focused beam of energy. That might enable a ghost to materialize. There's also a more abstract possibility: When two mirrors face each other, they create an infinite image—reflections within reflections. The series of reflections resembles a tunnel composed of light, descending deep within the glass. Since both light and ghosts are essentially electromagnetic energy, facing mirrors might produce a kind of energy portal through which entities can travel. You may find you can influence ghostly activity by changing the orientation of mirrors. If a haunted room contains two mirrors facing each other, move one to a different angle, then note any change. You might even be able to terminate, or enhance, a haunting by making such simple adjustments.

Using equipment is only one part of ghost research. The

other part is quite journalistic. As with any research, it is important to record written details about the location and activity. Your first step should be to conduct historical analysis. If you're investigating an old house, you might want to dig through records at the local library to find out about its past. To an extent, it seems each library organizes local records in their own unique way. But the librarian in charge of regional documents should be able to produce files for specific needs. For example, many libraries will have a folder devoted to old and historic homes or significant crimes in the area. Better yet, some libraries have a folder devoted to local haunts. Important regional materials are not usually accessible without a librarian's assistance, so be sure to ask for help. Old newspaper clippings can be invaluable, and are often the only source of documentation you may find.

Ghost hunters frequently find themselves at the courthouse researching death certificates, wills, and land deeds. Usually, these documents do not give thorough details, but can serve to prove basic background information, such as who owned a location or who died there and how. Studying wills can give you good leads for interview subjects. Wills can be used to trace family lines, and if a haunting is the product of an incident fifty years past, it can be necessary to track down family members for inside information. In the same fashion, longtime residents of the community, especially local historians, can also contribute priceless information. Historians can be located via library materials, and meeting local residents is often achieved by simply knocking on their doors or giving them a phone call. And don't ever forget about the Internet. After typing your subject into a search engine, like www.google.com, you might be amazed by what information pops up.

When researching incidents that may have spawned a

haunting, you must ultimately try to answer the six basic questions of journalism:

1. Who?
2. What?
3. When?
4. Where?
5. Why?
6. How?

The more knowledge you have about a location before the investigation, the better.

Upon arriving at an occupied locale, you should also interview anyone who may have information about the haunting. Obviously, firsthand experiences are best. In some cases, ghost hunters observe and measure the environment *before* getting information about the ghostly activity or property history. This assures that the investigators do not have any preconceived notions regarding their findings. Patrons paying for research often prefer this method. It is more compelling if, based upon your findings, *you* tell the owner the most active areas of the property before he or she tells you. Based upon the work involved, you must choose which method to use on a case-by-case basis. Later in the text, you will read a synopsis of how a typical investigation is conducted.

As you collect evidence, it is important to realize the difference between a *whole-real* experience and a *half-real* experience. I touched upon this concept when discussing naturals, but its implications are infinitely wider. Throughout this book, I've stressed the difference between subjective and objective evidence. To the individual, reality is a combination of both. It is the hybrid of what is actually there and what we perceive to be there. As a researcher, you must be able to quickly and easily identify each kind of experience. One half of reality is subjective or internal, the other half objective or external.

Let's say you look into a haunted room and don't see anything with your naked eyes. Then, you snap a digital photo and a ghost appears in the picture. This is considered a half-real experience. That's because it occurred in objective reality, but not your subjective perception. Therefore, we would technically call this a *half-real objective* experience.

On the other hand, perhaps you do see a ghost with your naked eyes, but snap a photo that shows nothing. This would be a *half-real subjective* experience. That's because it occurred in your subjective reality, but not the objective.

It's always better to have a half-real objective encounter. That's because objectivity is the pillar of science. Of course, the best type of experience to have would be a whole-real. If you see a ghost with your naked eye, then capture a photograph of it, you've had a whole-real experience, in which both halves, subjective and objective, were documented.

There are three types of whole-real experiences. Type one is when your objective evidence matches what you witnessed subjectively. Simply enough, if you see a white ghost with big purple eyes, then capture a picture of a white ghost with big purple eyes, that's a *whole-real type one.* Type two is when the objective does not match the subjective. For example, if you see a white ghost with big purple eyes, then get a photo that shows only orbs, that's a *whole-real type two.* Type three is a combination of type one and type two. In other words, if the objective matches the subjective, plus shows something extra, that's type three. That means if you only see a big white ghost with purple eyes, and you snap a picture that shows a big white ghost with purple eyes, plus orbs around it, that's a *whole-real type three.* By the same token, if you see orbs with your naked eyes, then get a photo of orbs *plus* an apparition, that's also type three. You could even go so far as to specify type-three subjective or type-three objective.

Once again:

1. **Half-real subjective:** When you subjectively perceive something that was not documented via objective means.
2. **Half-real objective:** When you perceive nothing subjectively, but obtain objective documentation.
3. **Whole-real:** When you are able to document an experience subjectively and objectively.
   Type one: When the subjective and objective appear the same.
   Type two: When the subjective and objective appear different.
   Type three: A combination of types one and two; when the subjective and objective match, but additional information is documented on either the objective or subjective side.

The typical ghost encounter, when the spirit is seen and then vanishes, would be a half-real subjective experience. Remember, calling something half-real does not mean it did not possess objective reality, but that it was not, or could not be, documented. The term *half-real* in no way demeans the legitimacy of a realistic experience. It is simply a necessary way of dividing the plethora of experiences into a scientifically manageable form.

Even though objective evidence provides the facts upon which you should draw conclusions, remember that facts alone will not tell the complete story. You must be capable of taking these facts and using logic to apply meaning to them. Finding two and two is one thing, putting two and two together is quite another. This is most relevant when it comes to the subject of defining the kind of ghostly activity you're observing. It is important to reiterate that ghostly activity, whether of a conscious nature or imprint, is primarily detected in the same scientific way: via anomalous electromagnetic energy fields. Differentiating between classes of activity is dependent upon the observed behavior of the phenomenon. Remember, nonconscious imprints will manifest *exactly* the same way each time, while the activity of conscious spirits is more unpredictable.

THE EQUIPMENT

A ghost hunter's toolbox can contain simple, inexpensive items, or more high-tech gadgetry. Most investigators start out small and then build technology with time. There is no minimum requirement for the amount of equipment you use. Obviously, the more you have, the more accurately you can narrow down your findings. Some ghost hunters use no equipment at all, only their senses. Using bare human senses will be covered later. But you must keep this in mind: Though using your senses to detect ghosts may garner personal satisfaction, it carries little weight as objective evidence. Since your senses are limited, I highly recommend relying on tools for your serious investigations.

Following is a list of basic equipment, big and small, that ghost hunters will find beneficial:

1. Notebook and writing utensil
2. Flashlight
3. Batteries
4. Watch
5. Compass
6. Electromagnetic field meter
7. Still camera

8. Video camera
9. Tape recorder
10. Infrared meter
11. Dowsing rods
12. Thermometer
13. Walkie-talkies
14. Cellular phone
15. Powder and black plastic
16. Night-vision scope
17. Audio enhancer
18. Electrostatic generator
19. Strobe light
20. Tone generator
21. First-aid kit
22. Beverage and snack

Following is an in-depth explanation of how each of these items can be used for ghost research.

NOTEBOOK AND WRITING UTENSIL

As with any research, taking notes is a must. Locations, dates, times, witnesses' names (and contact information), environmental conditions, and experiences should all be recorded. A notebook should be your constant companion on an investigation. Don't trust yourself to remember all the details. When others scrutinize your work, the thorough details will prove invaluable. Such items are also important in the delicate process of finding patterns and correlations. You may find it helpful to use forms to make sure you don't forget anything important. Sample forms are included in the appendices to this guide.

Some investigators prefer to use a miniature digital or cassette recorder (often voice activated) to take notes. Though this may be convenient, it is not advised. Haunted areas can house bizarre energies that will interfere with the way a recorder works. As you'll see later, this can be used to your benefit. However, for the purpose of taking research notes, such disruptions can prove detrimental. It's difficult to beat the effective simplicity of a pad or notebook and a pen or pencil.

FLASHLIGHT

A good flashlight is integral to ghost research. Most times, you will find yourself in dark places. It's actually best to keep two flashlights. Keep a small, lightweight unit in your pocket, and have a larger, bulkier one for more extended use (especially outdoors). The brighter and more durable the lights, the better. Since you'll be using other equipment, you may also want to invest in a hands-free light, such as the kind that straps to your head. A red filter or gel on your lens might also prove beneficial. In a dark setting, your eyes are less affected by red light. That means if you turn off the light, it takes less time for your eyes to adjust in the darkness. If you see a faintly glowing apparition and kill your red light to view it, those extra seconds are precious.

BATTERIES

You'd be surprised how many ghost researchers forget to take extra batteries on an investigation. Obviously, the batteries you bring will depend on what you're using. Of the devices listed in this guide, flashlights, tape recorders, watches, energy meters, night-vision scopes, and video and still cameras usually take batteries. Murphy's Law certainly applies to paranormal work. When you're right in the middle of some rare and profound phenomenon, the batteries will konk out. In fact, paranormal locations are known for inexplicably draining battery power. On ghost hunts, it's common for a camera display to show more than an hour's battery life remaining, then suddenly terminate. Perhaps ghosts draw energy from batteries.

On the other hand, in the middle of a haunting, devices that usually take batteries may work without them. In 2002, I was the producer and host of the First Annual Paranormal Conference at the Grove Park Inn Resort and Spa, in Asheville, North Carolina. At the event, we sold EMF meters that generate a high-pitched tone. Afterward, one couple went home with their new unit. Shortly thereafter, while the husband was away at work, the wife was startled when their meter, in another room, began going berserk. Upset by the noise, their dogs barked uncontrollably. The wife raced into the room, trying to figure out how to turn off the unit. In frustration, she ripped off the battery cover, only to find that the device had no batteries installed. There is no conventional explanation for such an occurrence.

It's not that uncommon to hear tales of electronics' inexplicably operating without power. This is especially the case with children's toys. I've heard many a chilling tale about "possessed" toys that spontaneously activate at night. In some cases, they have to be destroyed.

Nonetheless, as a ghost hunter, don't count on *your* equipment working without batteries. Most of the time, you'll experience quite the opposite.

WATCH

Recording the time of events is important in any field work. Knowing the time allows you to pinpoint the specific moment when something occurs. This can especially help you deduce patterns in activity. Of course, discovering patterns is a key to defining imprints. Variables, like the hour and stage of the moon, might play a role in imprinting. Oftentimes a particular scene may replay itself only when these conditions are right. For example, a phantasmal suicide might be reenacted on every full moon at three in the morning, just like the night it originally occurred.

In retrospect, you can also use time to research environmental data, such as temperature and humidity. This information can be found in old newspapers or by contacting the National Weather Service and inquiring about a specific day. Make sure you can view your watch in the dark. However, a display that constantly glows can be detrimental. Aside from being a distraction, it might also make it more difficult for your eyes to adjust to the dark when needed. Multiple investigators should synchronize their watches.

It is well known that spiritual activity sometimes stops watches and clocks. When the great inventor Thomas Edison died in 1931, it's said that all the clocks in his home and laboratory quit working. Be cognizant of this. If you find that your watch has stopped, note the time it occurred. Watches are delicate instruments, and powerful energies can overwhelm them.

COMPASS

A compass is the most basic tool for detecting strange magnetic and electromagnetic fields. Most people are quite comfortable using a compass. Since they are small, inexpensive, and easy to find, they are one of the most popular tools for beginners. To use one most effectively requires keen awareness and a steady hand.

Obviously, when all is normal, a compass needle points north. If the device is influenced by another energy field, the needle is affected. If the needle does not point north, or if it moves erratically, you are encountering some kind of unusual field. In some cases, the needle will actually spin, as if it's in the middle of a magnetic vortex. This is the simplest way to detect the presence of unseen spirits. If your compass isn't acting normal, something is awry. A compass is not nearly as sensitive as some of the electronic tools you can buy, but penny for penny, it's your best bargain.

As with all instruments, you must be careful to rule out conventional explanations. Magnetic fields can be created by the wiring in appliances and electronics, or by metal objects that have been magnetized. Of course, be sure to watch out for common magnets lying around.

ELECTROMAGNETIC FIELD METER

The serious ghost hunter will quickly find an electromagnetic field (or EMF) meter to be an essential tool (Illus. 10). They do exactly what it sounds like: give specific readings of electromagnetic energies. There are several compact, hand-held versions on the market. The cost of one usually ranges from around $50 to $250. For the average investigator, more expensive models are seldom worth the extra money. Read-out can be obtained in most any format, including a standard needle, LED indicators, digital, and an accompanying audio tone. When choosing an EMF meter, ones that detect DC fields are best. However, AC meters can work as well. The fields encountered by ghosts can at times switch just like an AC field. Therefore, either type of device can detect ghosts, but it's best to use AC meters to find and rule out artificial fields, and use DC meters for locating phantoms. That's because AC is used in most homes (it's what comes out of your wall outlet), and natural electrical fields are usually of the DC type.

10. Here are some basic meters used for paranormal research. *Photo courtesy Joshua P. Warren*

EMF meters generally provide readouts in units called "milliGauss." An average television usually gives off around 4 to 8 milliGauss from a foot away. Keeping this in mind will help you scale the impact of readings you get in the field. The higher-end meters can be adjusted for amazing sensitivity. Most EMF meters cannot detect the subtle energy given off by the human body. However, devices like the TriField Natural EM Meter can pick up humans from up to ten feet away. It can also be set to pick up radio waves and microwaves.

When using EMF meters in a haunted location, you want to look for erratic fields of energy with no physical source. The best of these are self-contained fields that hover in midair, gliding around an area, then disappearing. When you detect such a field, you should take a photograph. As you will see, an EMF meter and a camera are best used hand in hand.

The most challenging aspect of using EMF meters is ruling out artificial fields, created by electronics, wiring, and appliances. Anytime electricity runs through a wire, it creates a magnetic field around it, and our modern world is inundated with electrical technology. Some meters will filter out artificial fields automatically, reading only those created in the natural environment. However, in most cases, you'll have to know how to do this yourself. The key is the behavior of the field. Since fields created artificially by televisions, lights, computers, etc., are primarily the product of electricity running through their wires, they do not fluctuate. They always remain constant. The closer you are to the objects, the stronger and more stationary the fields. The farther away, the weaker and more inconsistent. However, fields associated with spectral activity fluctuate wildly and are usually temporary.

There are only two ways to get a fluctuating field when close to an electronic device. The first is by physically moving the meter back and forth, close then far, from the source. The second is if the electricity running through the wiring is not a constant stream. If the electricity is pulsing, like that in a blinking light, or an alarm sensor that sweeps an area at intervals, it will create a pulse of energy as well. Most devices only produce constant fields, though.

Nine times out of ten, *if a mysterious field is constant and stable, it's artificial; if it fluctuates erratically, it's paranormal.* With experience, you'll quickly become proficient in differentiating between the two. Most life-forms create inconsistent fields. Simply try to imagine the motions of a spirit moving around you, traveling about the location. When you detect paranormal fields, try to track them, following the motions of the ghost. You may find these contained masses of energy doing remarkable things: moving toward walls, then disappearing into them, or rising higher and higher until they seem to float away.

If you obtain a meter that's sensitive enough to pick up

your body's energy, experiment with how it perceives your body. Move around it and see how it responds. Then, place an electronic device near it and note that response. You will soon appreciate the distinct difference between the erratic fields given off by organic creatures and the more "mechanical" and predictable ones created by technology.

Some hot spots *always* have a wealth of bizarre electromagnetic energy. If you continually get fluctuations in an area, and you've ruled out all artificial causes, you may have a hot spot. The energy might be caused by a ghost, or could be a source of energy the ghost uses to materialize. Such masses of EMFs may be the product of geomagnetic activity or a large-scale artificial source, like power lines. Even though artificial and conventional types of energies are not paranormal themselves, they could still enhance, or somehow affect, the total electrical environment necessary for a ghost's materialization. Masses of artificial EMFs, from perhaps an electrical power box, might somehow be used by a spirit to aid in manifestation.

EMF meters can be purchased at many electrical supply outlets or through catalogs of electronic gadgetry. My team's web site, www.LEMURteam.com, has information on obtaining them online. Or, if you're the constructive type, you can build a basic EMF meter with relative simplicity. Here's how: First, obtain a volt meter. They're carried by most hardware and home improvement stores and generally run thirty to fifty dollars. Buy the most sensitive one you can find, AC or DC. Ideally, it should be able to pick up millivolts, or mVs (one mV is one-thousandth of a volt). Then, buy a long, thick nail. Next, buy the smallest-gauge insulated wire you can find. Coil this around the nail, heaping it as thickly as necessary, and making sure to keep the two ends free. The more wire, the more powerful your meter will be.

Once the wire is wrapped around the nail and secured, via glue or some similar means, attach each end of the wire to your volt meter's plugs. Whenever a field passes near your coil, it will induce a surge of electricity in the volt meter. To determine the specific sensitivity of the device, you'd have to know how many turns of wire you used. Considering that you probably won't have this information (after hundreds or thousands of manual turns), you won't be able to use your homemade meter for documenting specifics. However, the benefit to this method is that you have unlimited potential. The bigger you make the coil, the more sensitive it will be.

STILL CAMERA

In a serious investigation, it is important to have a still camera on hand. With our current level of technology, the best way to learn about a ghost is by getting a good picture of it. The kind of camera is not that important. A standard 35-mm camera works perfectly fine. However, digital cameras are the tool of choice for most. There are pros and cons to both kinds. A digital camera gives you instant feedback. That's a HUGE plus, since it allows you to react to a manifestation quickly without having to run to the drugstore to check your results. Digital cameras are also cheaper to operate. You can take shots for pennies a pic, and you can erase a worthless pic to make space for new ones. Also, most digital cameras are naturally sensitive to some infrared light. You can test this quality by viewing a common television remote control through your camera, then pushing a button on the remote. If your camera is sensitive to infrared, you should clearly see a light emerge from the remote, one that is invisible to your naked eyes. This means that a digital can pick up everything you see *plus* some of the infrared realm you can't see. One of the big downfalls of a digital camera is that it does not provide a negative to be examined.

A film camera is usually capable of producing higher-quality pictures, plus they have a negative. However, it costs more to use them, considering the price of film and developing. Worst of all, you don't get the instant feedback. Also, in order to pick up infrared light, you must use special film, and it takes more manual effort to set your camera correctly. With both digital and film cameras, if you want to capture infrared light *alone,* you must also use a filter that allows only that kind of light to pass through. However, with digitals you can use that filter alone, while with film you must have the filter and special infrared film.

Some ghost hunters prefer Polaroid instant cameras. Even though they produce a photograph faster than traditional film, it still takes a few minutes. This is SLOW compared to a digital, which can show you the result in a second or two. Some ghost hunters believe the Polaroids are more sensitive to spiritual energies. However, the pictures cost more than a dollar a shot.

Here's a quick comparison between digital and film:

Digital Cameras
Pros: Instant feedback, cheaper to use, naturally sensitive to some infrared and ultraviolet.

Cons: Produces no negative, usually not as high quality as film.

Film Cameras
Pros: Usually higher quality than digital, produces a negative for examination.

Cons: No instant feedback, more expensive to use, more difficult to capture infrared or ultraviolet.

Most people who choose to use film for ghost hunts do so because of the negative. They perceive their photos as having more credibility. However, in many ways, it's just as easy to hoax a film picture as it is a digital. Therefore, when you weigh all the pros and cons, it seems clear that digital cameras are best. This is also due to the method by which they interpret the subject.

Film contains a layer of chemicals that is sensitive to light. This layer has crystals that undergo a chemical change when light hits them. The light from the subject enters the lens and has direct contact with the negative. That may be why some describe film pictures as being "warmer" than digital—because the subject makes a direct imprint.

Digital cameras work differently. The light from the subject hits an electronic piece called a "charged coupled device," or CCD. This unit interprets the electrons of the light as pre-programmed colors. Therefore, the image is not a direct impression of the subject in the same manner as film. This may be a more suitable means of ghost photography, though. Spirits manifest in an electrical form, and digital cameras are more sensitive to interpreting such energy. All light contains electrical potential, but not all electrical potential produces light. A CCD can take a charge that does not produce light—thereby being invisible to a film camera—yet still create an image of it digitally.

If you do choose to use a film camera, the more sensitive the film, the better. Therefore, 800 ASA or higher is recommended. Regardless of whether you use film or digital, shutter speed is important due to the mechanics of ghost photography. Everyone wants to see a ghost and photograph it—to have a whole-real experience. However, most of the time, you'll have a half-real objective experience, where you don't see anything when the photo is taken but a ghostly image appears in the picture. How can this be?

Think about an electrical fan. When the blades are not moving, they are easy to see. However, the faster they spin, the more transparent they become. At full speed, the individual blades are completely invisible (Illus. 11). This happens because the light reflecting from the blades is broken up at an oscillation faster than the brain can perceive. Perhaps spirits can appear in a similar fashion. If ghosts occupy an appropriate frequency, they may oscillate at a faster rate than the human eye can detect. Therein lies the benefit of photography.

11. To the naked eye, the individual fan blades are invisible. *Photo courtesy Joshua P. Warren*

If one photographs the spinning fan blades, they may develop partially or still look invisible. But the photographer can control the outcome by adjusting the shutter speed. The shutter speed is the amount of time the camera exposes the film to the subject. If spinning blades are photographed with a low shutter speed, it will develop as a blur. The faster the shutter speed, the clearer the image of the blades. A quick shot captures the propeller in one fleeting position, whereas a slow shot is exposed long enough to capture the blades in several positions—thus creating the blur. If the shutter speed is fast enough, the blades actually appear to stand still (Illus. 12). This somewhat duplicates the experience of photographing a ghost. To the naked eye, the blades are invisible. When photographed at a high shutter speed, they become visible. The invisible becomes visible by using photography appropriately.

12. When photographed with the proper settings, the blades become visible. *Photo courtesy Joshua P. Warren*

The effect can also be observed using a strobe light. These devices duplicate the action of a camera shutter, flashing on and off fast enough to isolate an image your brain can perceive. If you put a strobe on a spinning fan, the blades will appear to stand still once the proper strobing speed is used. By this token, if a strobe were invented that could flash at the correct rate, it might make the spiritual world visible to the naked eye.

If the comparison is accurate, it seems the best ghost photos can be taken with higher shutter speeds. One should also note that higher shutter speeds demand more light on the subject. This is because the subject is not being exposed long, so it needs more light to appear distinctly. A subject in dim lighting looks brighter if a slower shutter speed is used, exposing it longer. All this shutter speed business aside, plenty of good ghost photos are taken every day using standard photo techniques—no different from photographing a day at the park. Basic point-and-shoot cameras can turn out great ghost pictures, as well as more manual, professional models. The key is, as usual, experimentation. Regardless of the means, to obtain a good ghost photo, the most important factor is being in the right place at the right time.

You might also try asking entities if you may take their photo before snapping off a shot. In some cases, it does indeed seem to make a difference. This suggests that the entity can have some measure of control over how photogenic it is. Also, once in a while, spontaneously take a quick shot behind you, over your shoulder. You could find that a wraith is following you around.

Advanced ghost hunters may want to learn more about infrared and ultraviolet photography. Even though using a digital camera might give you some extra infrared insight, the electromagnetic spectrum is far fuller. In fact, digital cameras see only into the "near infrared" realm, meaning the portion closest to visible light. The visible electromagnetic spectrum spans from the color red to the color violet. Just past red lies the infrared realm, and just past violet lies the ultraviolet realm (Illus. 13). But light contains much more. You can reach back to grammar school to remember how a wave of electromagnetic energy is designed. It's just like a wave in the ocean. It has a part that rises, the crest, and a part that drops low, the trough. In a beam of energy, the distance from one crest to the next determines the wavelength. The frequency is how many wavelengths pass a fixed point in a specific period of time. As wavelength grows longer, frequency is lower. As wavelength grows shorter, frequency is higher. We measure wavelengths in nanometers (nm), or one-billionth of a meter. Visible light ranges from approximately 400 to 700 nm, 400 being the color violet and 700 being red. The human retina can be sensitive to ultraviolet light as short as 350 nm; however, fluids in the eye absorb this wavelength, therefore no ultraviolet is seen. Also, some people's eyes can see high-intensity infrared light as long as 1,050 nm, but it appears as bright flashes. Whether or not one can see into these transitional wavelengths, and to what degree, apparently depends on the genetic design of the eye. Have you ever seen a flash of light, then were unable to find what caused it? Something in the infrared realm may have passed by quickly. Note that young people can see more than older people because the density of

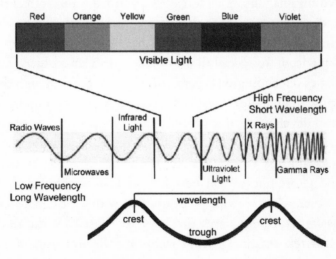

13. The electromagnetic spectrum. *Courtesy Robert McGhee*

the eyes' components increases with age, decreasing the type of light that can pass through.

On one end of the electromagnetic spectrum, you have long wavelength, low frequency radio waves. If the wavelengths shorten a bit, and the frequency increases, you get microwaves. Even shorter wavelengths with higher frequency produce infrared. From there, it passes through the visible light and into ultraviolet, with a short wavelength and high frequency, then to X rays and gamma rays. The energy that comes from a harmless flashlight can kill you if sped up to a higher level, like gamma rays. Slow it down, and you've got deadly microwaves. It's all the same substance, but it creates varied effects depending on its form.

Each type of energy represents a facet of reality to be explored. Humans tend to view their perspective of reality as the only one. However, penguins can see ultraviolet light. What does their reality look like? What can they see that we cannot? Exploring these other realms of light is important. Anything that allows us to explore a broader range than the naked senses perceive is valuable.

In order to photograph these other realms, you must usually incorporate special films, filters, and various other technologies depending on where you explore. Even though this is truly an arena for advanced researchers, it is an important part of developing your knowledge.

Regardless of the method of photography you use, there are certain tips you should keep in mind when in the field. Good ghost photos can be taken with or without a flash. However, when viewing pictures made with a flash, take into consideration light flares that may be caused by the flash. Such flares, emanating from white or reflective objects, are commonly mistaken for ghostly images. Light can reflect especially from raindrops, fog, or anything too close to the camera. You should consider removing any small straps from the camera as well. Dangling straps often fall at the edge of the lens, unknown to the photographer. In a developed photo, portions of straps can look like bright, linear streaks of light. This is known as the "camera strap phenomenon." However, it includes more than just camera straps. A hair, piece of fuzz, or anything very close to the lens can create a deceiving effect. Also, try to avoid firing multiple flashes at once, as when several people are photographing the same thing. The additional flashes can create strange and contaminating optical effects. If you are part of a team of photographers, it's good to call "flash" before taking a photo. That way, each person will be warned, and cross-contamination can be avoided. Of course, smoking on the scene is a taboo as well. A wisp of smoke can look a lot like a ghostly form. Even your breath on a cold night can take on a ghostly effect.

With experience, you'll find that all manner of images can be obtained in connection with ghosts. However, there are three types that are most common: orbs, mists, and bodied apparitions.

Orbs

These are any unexplainable circles or balls of light (Illus. 14). Earlier in the text, we discussed the possibility that phantoms may sometimes travel in this shape since it's the most energy-efficient. Even so, this type of image is the one most easily caused by conventional means. A drop of rain, a speck of dirt or dust on the lens, an insect, or a reflection can all cause orb-like images. It's good to intentionally photograph these things so you'll know what they look like. A trained, experienced eye can differentiate between normal and anomalous orbs. Just be sure to exercise caution. The most compelling orbs are those caught on video. They can move with lightning speed or slowly bounce along in a curious way. They can pass through objects, and the intensity of their illumination can change. Some of the most interesting photos show orbs partially hidden behind objects in the photo. This shows that they're far away from the camera, unlike a speck of dust or a spot on the lens.

Often, orbs appear to have a nucleus, just like a cell. The nucleus might be surrounded by "bands"—concentric circles emerging from it. In fact, it might almost appear like an onion that's been chopped in half.

Although orbs are frequently captured in the visible realm, it seems they are most active in the infrared environment. Because of this, digital cameras are especially good at capturing them. Some of the most spectacular orb activity I've ever seen has been captured with infrared technology. Half-real objective experiences often include orbs picked up by digital cameras, otherwise invisible to the naked eye.

14. Is this large orb a reflection, an artifact, or something else? *Photo courtesy Brian Irish*

Since ghosts have an electrostatic field, it makes sense that particles from the atmosphere would be trapped in that field and form a tiny clump of particles that marks the phantom's presence. Could some of these orblike specks be a ghost's flying-dust footprint?

We cannot conclusively say that paranormal orbs are ghosts. However, they often appear abundantly at haunted locations. Therefore, there seems to be some definite connection between ghostly activity and orbs. The exact nature of that relationship is still being explored.

Mists

These are nebulous masses that appear in photos (Illus. 15). They look like thick smoke. Though usually white, a mist can be any color. In many cases, mists demonstrate no organized structure at all. In other cases, they seem to form rough shapes, like bodies or faces. That certainly does not mean such

15. This thick mist shows form and texture.
Photo courtesy Amanda Annarino

images are truly within them. Mists are very much like clouds. You and I could look at the same one and each see something different. It's a good example of the brain's tendency to make order out of chaos, to connect lines where they might not be connected; in short, to see the man in the moon.

A mist could be an apparition whose body has broken the mold of its old, physical self. Mists that appear somewhat abstract and somewhat like a being might indicate phantoms in a state of transition from one form to another. Or a mist might sometimes be a physical by-product of a ghost's presence—some effect on the environment we don't yet understand. In some cases, they might actually consist of moisture. Mists frequently appear to be in motion, swirling about from one place to the next (Illus. 16).

16. Is this mist moving into the man or out of him? *Photo courtesy Amanda Annarino*

Like orbs, these can be easily created by conventional means. Smoke from a cigarette, fog, condensation from your breath, condensation on the lens, and other similar culprits frequently deceive investigators. Keep this in mind: Misty images caused by airborne particles usually look rather thin, flat, and consistent. Paranormal mists tend to have more dimension, depth, and shape, and can display wild, inconsistent patterns. As always, it's good to photograph smoke, fog, dust, and condensation so you'll see how these conventional "mists" appear.

Bodied Apparitions

These clearly show part, or all, of a well-defined ghost. At face value, they display indisputable images. In most circumstances, these images are either real or intentionally faked; there are few other possibilities. A full-bodied apparition is the cream of the crop.

One of the most famous photographs of a full-bodied apparition is the Brown Lady of Raynham Hall (Illus. 17). It was taken in Norfolk, England, in 1936. Raynham Hall is a grand manor, and two magazine photographers were taking pictures of its architecture when the phantom appeared, floating down the staircase. Upon seeing the ghost, they frantically snapped the legendary photograph. It's one of those rare cases when a whole-real type-one experience was documented. Throughout the decades, this picture and its negative have been subjected to extensive scrutiny by photography experts. However, no evidence of trickery has ever been found.

A partial-bodied apparition is also quite compelling. In some cases, a body part will appear, as if hovering in midair. At other times, a torso and head, or perhaps only legs, or virtually any fragmented aspect of a being, can appear. Photos of partial-bodied apparitions are far more common than full-bodied ones.

17. The Brown Lady
of Raynham Hall.
*Photo courtesy Fortean
Picture Library*

Whether you obtain a picture of an orb, mist, or bodied apparition, these anomalous images can appear as almost any color. I'm often asked what these colors mean. Are black ones evil? Are good ones white? It's probably ridiculous to judge a ghost entirely by its color. It's like saying a black person is evil while a white one is good; a kind of spectral racism. On the other hand, if color does indicate anything about the ghost, it probably works along the lines of seeing an aura. Obviously, color indicates the frequency and wavelength of electromagnetism, as well as temperature (for example, red being cooler, while blue is hotter and white is hottest). From that perspective, color may have relevance.

Taking good ghost photos is certainly exciting, but using them as proof is a different story. A picture is just a picture.

An image alone will never conclusively prove anything. Though it may prove something to the photographer, it will always hold limited impact on the scientific community. It's too easy to fake an image. Plus, light does unusual things. It reflects off things, distorts, and is ultimately viewed as a wild card. That's why you should use photos to lead you in the right directions—places where you can confirm more objective activity via means like meters. However, there is a way you can insure your photographs hold a bit more water. It's 3-D photography.

When you're looking at an image on a flat piece of paper, lots of details are indiscernible. It's difficult to tell how far objects are from the camera. Are you looking at something small right next to the lens, or something huge a good distance away? 3-D technology can help solve this problem. 3-D duplicates how your eyes see the world. It's the product of taking two pictures of the same subject from slightly different angles, mimicking the perspectives of the human eyes. When these two images are combined, it creates a single, depthful image, a miniature representation of reality.

A 3-D camera has two lenses (Illus. 18). When you snap a photo, you end up with two pictures of the same subject, each from close but different positions. Usually, these two pictures are placed into a special viewer. It optically merges them together. When you look at them, you see 3-D, a subjective experience. You can buy a 35-mm 3-D camera and viewer (like the Argus 3D Stereo camera) for around a hundred dollars. They can be obtained or ordered through many camera supply stores, or by visiting sites online like www.3Dstereo.com. Or, you can make one by simply placing two cameras side by side and snapping them both at once. The cameras' lenses should be placed 6.5 cm apart, each slightly tilted toward the subject.

18. A 3-D still camera. *Photo courtesy Joshua P. Warren*

A 3-D picture of the Empire State Building in New York has been included (Illus. 19). Though each picture, side-by-side, may look identical to the other, they are indeed different. Despite the fact that the pictures are meant to be placed in a viewer, some people can see the 3-D effect with their naked eyes. How about you?

Hold the two pictures of the building about a foot from your face. Now cross your eyes, and try to get the two to merge into one. It might be unfocused at first, but if you hold your gaze, the focus should clear up, leaving you with a nice 3-D effect.

If that technique doesn't work, here's another one. Again, hold the pictures about a foot from your face. Now lift up your finger between your face and the book. Look past your finger at the book. Upon looking past your finger, it should optically "divide" into two fingers. Once you see two fingers, move your finger back and forth until "each finger" lines up

19. A stereoscopic photo of the Empire State Building. *Photo courtesy Joshua P. Warren*

with the center of each picture. Now, look back at your finger—it will turn into one finger again. However, in the background, the two pictures should now have a third image between them. Keep your eye on the point in space occupied by your finger, then slowly lower the finger, careful to maintain your gaze. If you can hold your eyes at that state, the "third picture" should be 3-D. Again, to fix bad focus, just wait a moment and it should clear up. Have difficulty? Then try the second 3-D picture, a photo I took of a cave entrance—the tourists in the foreground especially stick out (Illus. 20).

You can also take a 3-D picture using one camera if you snap off a shot, then slide it over 6.5 cm and take another shot of the same thing. However, you can photograph only a subject sitting still in this way. Obviously, a subject in motion wouldn't work. Therefore, this method is not beneficial for most ghost investigations. It can be used to document your location, though.

The best thing about 3-D is that it allows you to rule out

20. A stereoscopic photo of a cave entrance.
Photo courtesy Joshua P. Warren

many more-conventional explanations for your anomalous image. If you find some white mass on your photo, and it's captured in 3-D, you can prove it's not a reflection, something smeared on the lens, or a flaw in the developing process. Those things are 2-D. It's also far more difficult to convincingly hoax the subtleties of a 3-D picture. As such, an anomaly captured in 3-D is worth far more than one captured by conventional imagery.

During the 1800s, when spiritualism was running rampant, lots of people took fake ghost photos. In fact, it became big business. Back then, you couldn't snap off a picture in a second. Instead, the subject would have to sit still for several minutes while his or her image was fully absorbed by the negative. During the course of this period, if someone walked into the photo for several seconds, then walked out, that person would appear as an eerie translucent figure. Most of the public was ignorant as to how photography worked. Therefore, when such an anomaly appeared, people were shocked. Photographers quickly realized the value of these "ghost" photographs. Sometimes, when a subject was posing for a photo, the photographer would have an assistant, dressed in a white sheet or some other ghoulish wardrobe, silently creep out behind the customer and stand for a bit before slinking off. When the picture was developed, it looked like a specter stood behind the subject. Naïve patrons would believe it was the spirit of a departed loved one, and suddenly the photograph became much more valuable to the individual. This unscrupulous business practice gave ghost photography a bad name for many years.

It is now easier than ever to fake ghost photos. That's why the photographer's overall credibility is so important. Even though illegitimate pictures can be fabricated, that does not demean the value of the authentic ones. James Cameron was able to realistically fake the sinking of the *Titanic* in his film. However, that doesn't mean the ship didn't really sink in 1912. Weigh all evidence carefully.

Now, as our technology expands year after year, the public captures an ever-growing number of phantasmal images. We can take pictures faster and cheaper than ever before. And we now have easier access to photographing the infrared and ultraviolet realms than ever before. Cameras allow us to see things we cannot see—things that move too fast or occupy a section of reality outside the scope of our natural observation. For that, they are incredibly important. They can literally serve as our eyes into the spirit world.

VIDEO CAMERA

Video cameras are wonderful for documenting an entire investigation (Illus. 21). A research team can greatly benefit from a skilled videographer. If a ghost does materialize, the footage will be invaluable. Though video is sensitive to the same range of light as human eyes, it can also pick up unseen presences, as still cameras can. Video cameras use a CCD, like digital still cameras. Therefore, they too are sensitive to the near-infrared realm. However, some video cameras on the market excel in that respect, especially the Sony Digital Handycam.

The twentieth century saw one of the biggest lunges forward in paranormal research due to video cameras with night-vision modes. Although the CCD on an ordinary camera can see into the infrared realm, cameras with night features can see far deeper into that realm. Apparently, all CCD cameras have this potential. However, manufacturers place a filter over the CCD that cuts out most of the infrared. This is so it won't distort imagery as perceived by the human eye. Cameras with a night feature have a switch that physically

21. Video cameras are an integral tool, especially those with infrared night-vision features. *Photo courtesy Joshua P. Warren*

removes this filter, allowing the user to enjoy the full benefits of the CCD's sensitivity. Unfortunately, CCDs are not as sensitive to ultraviolet light as infrared. Therefore, it's still challenging to document that realm conveniently. Since these cameras have hit the consumer market, a plethora of anomalies have appeared most prominently in the infrared environment. The most outstanding of these are orbs.

In many ways, a video camera can be used like a still camera. It's more or less a digital camera that takes thirty pictures per second. If you think of it that way, it will greatly improve your ability to use it effectively. Of course, the downfall is that it doesn't freeze something your eyes may have missed. Instead, it keeps moving right along, more similar to how the brain sees the world.

Another benefit of videography is infinite video imaging, or IVI. This is a controversial technique of electronically capturing ghostly images. It requires a video camera, television, and (depending on the television) a VCR. At a haunted location, you take a video camera and hook its audio-video output into the audio-video input on the back of a television. If the television is an older model, it might not have inputs. If this is the case, you may have to hook a VCR to the television, then connect the video camera's output to the VCR's input. Ultimately, you want an arrangement where whatever you point the camera toward appears on the television screen live. This is the kind of setup you commonly see in the electronics sections of department stores when you walk up and find yourself on television.

Once everything is hooked up properly, you turn the camera toward the television screen. The screen immediately displays a barrage of colors, designs, and abstract imagery. You are in essence capturing an infinite image. Then, you hit the Record button on the camera. After allowing the camera to tape this infinite image for several minutes or more, stop the camera and watch the footage.

Some researchers claim that supernatural forms may appear upon playback, especially if the tape is paused at the right time or played in slow motion. There is no clear explanation for why this may work. However, it's basically the equivalent of placing two mirrors in a position to face each other. You end up with a tunnel of images descending into some technological abyss. Using this method, the infinite effect can be recorded, though. It is a strange technique that is certainly worthy of more research.

Tape Recorder

Tape recorders are useful for what are generally known as "electronic voice phenomenon," or EVP. Basically, you set up a tape recorder, with a fresh tape, in a haunted location. The location is then left undisturbed for the length of the recording. When the tape is played back, bizarre noises may be recorded, including actual voices from the spirit realm.

When using standard audio tape, it's possible that these sounds and voices are directly imprinted by the spiritual dimension on the electromagnetically sensitive medium. However, this may not be the case with digital recording devices. Though one of the most widely used methods of ghost detection, there is little understanding of how this remarkable phenomenon works.

Some claim to be able to communicate with the "other side" by asking questions, then letting the tape roll. Upon playback, the questions may be answered by an eerie, static-sounding voice. For some reason, EVP often sounds as if it's trembling. There's a certain sense of oscillation in the sound, and that may provide a clue that helps us someday understand the phenomenon better.

Of course, audio recording devices are wonderful for documenting noises that *can* be heard by the human ear as well. Just keep in mind that, for a successful session, the tape must be fresh, and the area must be left undisturbed. Otherwise, the slightest murmur can be mistaken for an otherworldly sound.

INFRARED METER

Infrared meters are similar to EMF meters. They are compact, handheld units. But instead of detecting and measuring EMFs, they display levels of infrared activity. These meters are most useful when applied to infrared photography. The instruments can locate masses of invisible energy so they can be photographed. One must be careful when using such meters, however. They pick up humans, animals, and sources of heat, usually up to 150 feet away.

Hunters use infrared meters to locate downed game in the wild; they are commonly called "game scans." You can purchase them at sporting goods stores or through sportsman's catalogs for around a hundred dollars.

DOWSING RODS

Dowsing rods are rather controversial instruments for detecting ghostly electromagnetic energies. The word *dowsing* brings to mind water-seeking old-timers searching the fields with a forked stick. However, that traditional image of dowsing has little to do with our application of this technique. As opposed to a stick, a ghost hunter's rods can be made with a metal coat hanger.

To make dowsing rods, you must cut a metal coat hanger in three places (Illus. 22). The first cut should be in the middle of the bottom section of the hanger. The other two cuts should be made halfway up each side of the hanger. You may discard the section containing the hook. What remains are two stiff wires bent at roughly a 45-degree angle. You should then bend each of the wires to a 90-degree angle. You will end up with two L-shaped wires. These are your rods.

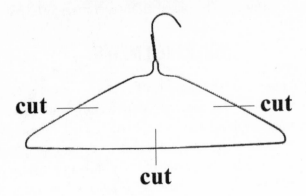

22. When cut properly, a metal coat hanger makes effective dowsing rods. *Photo courtesy Joshua P. Warren*

The shorter ends of the rods are the handles. You should place a wire in each hand, holding them like two pistols. Then, bring the knuckles of each hand together, positioning the wires side-by-side. Your grip should be loose, allowing the rods to swing freely (Illus. 23).

You can use the dowsing rods by walking around a haunted location with them. Make no attempt to move them voluntarily. In fact, take precautions to prevent them from moving due to air currents or your stride. Being made of metal, the rods will react if they come into contact with strong fields of magnetic or electromagnetic energy. They will swing wildly, or, upon coming atop the source of a field, they often cross each other. You can experiment with their behavior using a regular magnet. Dowsing rods can therefore be used somewhat like EMF meters and compasses: to help locate energy fields.

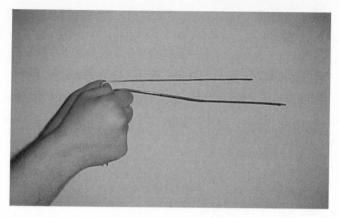

23. Dowsing rods in use. *Photo courtesy Joshua P. Warren*

To make your dowsing rods more efficient, cut narrow sections of PVC pipe (standard, plastic plumbing pipe, found at hardware stores) and slide them over the handles. This produces a barrier between your flesh and the wires, lessening your influence on their movement and creating lower friction for more fluid swinging. With experience, you will learn how to interpret them most effectively. Expert dowsers say the movements can indicate more than just abstract fields of energy.

One word of caution: Be careful when using this device. Remember, you're walking around with wires sticking out! Don't jab them into someone or something. Keeping that in mind, be sure not to use them under dark and similarly dangerous conditions.

THERMOMETER

When exploring haunted grounds, ghost hunters frequently refer to "cold spots." These are simply isolated and seemingly self-contained patches of air that feel significantly cooler than the surrounding environment. The difficulty with understanding cold spots lies in differentiating between subjective and objective temperatures. For example, one may feel cold from ions brushing the flesh. However, just because the person may feel cold, that does not mean the temperature is actually lower. One's body temperature can drop with nervousness or fear. It's not uncommon for one person in a room to be cold while another is hot.

When a ghost tries to materialize, it draws energy from the environment. Heat is a form of energy. Cold spots may be caused by spirits who take in the heat energy around them but fall short of enough to appear. There is no solid explanation for why else the presence of a spirit should cause a drop in the external temperature. However, such phenomena are commonly reported by ghost hunters. For purposes of observation, it's good to place a thermometer in an area where ghosts often materialize. The more information you have about your surroundings, the better.

To take temperature readings effectively, I highly recom-

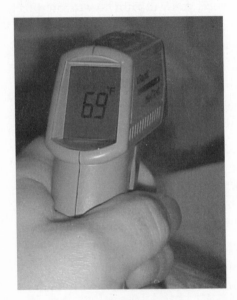

24. A remote temperature gauge provides instant feedback. *Photo courtesy Joshua P. Warren*

mend purchasing a noncontact thermal gauge (Illus. 24). These are devices that can give you the temperature of an area or surface instantly, up to hundreds of feet away in some cases. They interpret the infrared emanations from an object and are able to calculate an accurate temperature immediately. Good units can be obtained for fifty to one hundred dollars from electronics or hardware stores. When it comes to serious work, no paranormal researcher should be without one.

WALKIE-TALKIES

If you have more than one person on an investigation, walkie-talkies are valuable, especially when researching a large area. If someone is experiencing phenomena, other witnesses can be called immediately. Just be sure that broadcast energy does not contaminate your results, especially if you're using a device that can pick up radio waves. Sometimes, ghosts may even communicate via the radios! Also, haunted locations will at times produce odd radio interference that can be detected with your units.

CELLULAR PHONE

In secluded locations, it doesn't hurt to have a link to the outside world. As with two-way radios, be aware that some kinds of meters will pick up cellular phones. If using such equipment, you should keep your phone turned off until needed. Obviously, you never want to disrupt your energy readings.

POWDER AND BLACK PLASTIC

Ghost hunters have long tried to capture the "footprints" of spirits, or at least some physical trace of their presence. One of the simplest methods is to sprinkle white powder over a

dark floor. If a field passes through, it might disturb the powder, leaving a mark or impression of some kind.

The easiest way to do this is by cutting down a side and
bottom of a black plastic trash bag, thus creating a large, flat
piece of material. Then sprinkle a thin layer of flour or talcum
powder over the bag. The layer should be just thick enough
to cover the black surface. Place the setup in a hot spot, and
leave it undisturbed. When checked later on, a phantom's
energy may have disturbed the powder. Using the plastic,
cleanup is easy. Be sure that others know about the setup,
otherwise you're liable to end up with sneaker prints.

NIGHT-VISION SCOPE

A night-vision scope, often used by hunters and by surveil-
lance specialists, has two uses in the field (Illus. 25). First, it
allows a researcher to see in the dark without creating light
pollution. This can help to preserve the integrity of ghost

25. A basic night-vision scope. *Photo courtesy
Joshua P. Warren*

photos or any light-sensitive results. Second, like video and digital cameras, they will allow you to see into the infrared realm (Illus. 26). The extent to which you can see depends upon the quality of your device. Generally, cheaper models are considered "generation 0." Better devices are "first generation," mediocre ones are "second," and the highest caliber is "third generation." However, all models should be able to see the otherwise invisible beam of infrared energy flashing from a television or VCR remote control. A high-quality one can even see heat energy rising off objects. The scope's generation should be marked on the device or included on its packaging. One without a marking is probably generation 0.

Night-vision scopes can range from around $150 to many thousands. The more expensive devices are usually binocular goggles that can be strapped to the wearer's head. Some researchers claim that only the high-end models are worth investing in for spectral observation. However, any scope

26. When viewed through a night-vision scope, a remote control's infrared beam is visible.
Photo courtesy Joshua P. Warren

makes a nice addition to your ghost hunting tools. They can be used indoors or outdoors, under any dark conditions. Just be sure not to use them in bright light or you might damage their sensitive optics.

There was a time when these scopes could be obtained only from sporting goods stores or from wild-game hunters' catalogs. Now, you can even find them at places like Wal-Mart from time to time. There is no particular brand you should seek. As is usually the case, the more expensive the better.

AUDIO ENHANCER

Haunted locations are often filled with unexplained noises. Because of this, a device that enhances low sounds can be valuable (Illus. 27). Such instruments do have limited use, though. If you're investigating a location like an operating hotel or occupied home, it might be difficult to separate any paranormal noises from natural ones. If the environment is relatively quiet, though, such audio enhancement can be of great benefit. Many ghost hunters attach their audio enhancement devices to their tape and digital recorders, allowing them to document the sounds. This makes it possible to later magnify them as well.

Today's market is full of affordable software for manipulating sound files. Once you transfer a recording onto a computer, you can enhance and analyze it in a variety of ways. The human ear can only hear sounds from around 20 to 20,000 hertz. You can compare that to a dog, which can hear up to 40,000, and cats, which can hear up to 60,000. Smaller creatures, like rodents, are able to hear more than 100,000 hertz. Dogs' and cats' ability to perceive the paranormal realms has long been a staple of legend and lore. Perhaps this idea has credence, considering that we know they are receptive to information far beyond the range of human senses.

27. An audio enhancer and recorder. *Photo courtesy Joshua P. Warren*

By manipulating recordings, you can hear sounds you were unable to hear at the time of recording. Upon playback, if you speed up a recording, it will help you hear subsonic or infrasonic sounds: those too low for your ears to perceive. If you slow one down, it will help you hear ultrasonic sounds: those too high for your ears to perceive.

Regardless of how you handle audio recordings after the fact, audio enhancers will help you attain as much information as possible on the original recording. Generally, audio enhancers consist of headphones and an ultrasensitive microphone. Any device that magnifies sounds can be used, though. You can often find surprisingly effective units in toy stores for around $30. Professional models, used for surveillance by private investigators, might run around $150 to $200. They can be obtained through many catalogs of electronic gadgetry or easily found online. I especially like the Bionic Ear & Booster, available from Silver Creek

Industries in Manitowoc, Wisconsin (www.SilverCreek-Industries.com).

ELECTROSTATIC GENERATOR

This is certainly a tool for the advanced ghost hunter. Proper use of these devices also calls for some knowledge of electrical physics.

If the materialization of ghosts is dependent upon electrostatic charges, then any device that breaks up natural electrical bonds, thereby spraying ions into the air, should enhance ghostly activity. There are generators that pour an abundance of ions into the environment. Using them might be like providing precut building blocks that a spirit can use to materialize. They will not create activity, but they might heighten activity already taking place. These tools can only be used indoors since they can only affect a confined space of air.

As mentioned earlier, the Van de Graaff and Wimshurst/Bonetti machines are two of the best generators to use. They each can pour hundreds of thousands of volts into the air, and such generators are utilized primarily by simply allowing them to run for a while at a haunted indoor location. The Van de Graaff is a metal spheroid that rests atop an insulated base. A rubber belt running inside builds up positive charges that emanate from the ball. The Wimshurst/Bonetti consists of two upright, parallel disks made of glass or plastic. The disks counterrotate and are able to separate charges, taking electrons (negative charges) to one electrode while delivering protons (positive charges) to another.

The Wimshurst/Bonetti is superior to the Van de Graaff because, though they both create high voltage (or amount of electricity), it produces more current (or power). Regardless

of the type of device you use, you should attach a metal needle or nail to the electrode, or electrodes, where the charges
build. This will make it easier for the charges to pour into the
air, since they more easily escape sharp points. It doesn't matter how you attach the nail or needle, so long as it's touching
the electrode, or electrodes, of the device.

For best results, run a dehumidifier in a room for several
hours before the ghost investigation. This draws moisture out
of the air, allowing the ions you produce to work more effectively. Otherwise, the charges will leak away into the air's
water. Then, carry out the investigation as planned with the
generator(s) running the entire time. An easy way to test the
air's level of humidity is by taking a piece of wool or fur and
rubbing it briskly on a piece of PVC pipe for thirty seconds.
Then bring the pipe near your face. If it has a strong charge,
you will feel the field press against your face, pulling your
hair toward it. The stronger the field, the drier the air and the
better the conditions to see a materialization.

You can also purchase small machines that spray ions
(usually negative) into the air for cleansing purposes. Such
charges pull debris from the air and create ozone gas in the
vicinity. Ozone kills many bacteria. Though the amount of
charges they produce is usually too small to benefit ghost
research, they are still better than no such device at all. The
bigger, the better. These small devices are sometimes called
"negative ion generators" or "ion air purifiers" and can be
obtained in many houseware stores or from websites like
www.indoorpurifiers.com.

Another device I should mention is the Tesla Coil.
Invented by electrical genius Nikola Tesla, the Tesla Coil
setup consists of a transformer, capacitor, spark gap, and pri-
mary/secondary coils of wire. It runs off very high voltage,
and produces high-frequency electrical emanations as well as

ionization. Scientists do not presently understand every way in which Tesla Coils influence the environment. However, heightened supernatural activity has been reported when they are in use. Tesla Coils can be very dangerous and should be handled only by those experienced with high-voltage electrical paraphernalia. You may want to note that for many years small, compact Tesla Coils have been sold as "Violet Ray Machines." The marketers claim therapeutic value can be gained by applying electrical charges to the body.

Versions of these devices can be ordered from the Edmund Scientific catalog (note: they sell only manual Wimshurst machines). They also carry a highly recommended book on the subject of electrostatics called *Homemade Lightning*, by R. A. Ford. You can request their catalog by calling 800-728-6999.

STROBE LIGHT

In the section regarding ghost photography, I explained how a strobe light can duplicate the effect of a camera shutter. As they flash, they isolate images that would otherwise move too fast for the human brain to perceive. You can easily demonstrate this by shining a strobe at a moving fan. As you adjust different strobe rates, you'll see the fan blades in differing stages. In the same way, they might help you see *other* things around you that move too fast to perceive.

During an investigation, it's beneficial to turn on a strobe light in a hot spot while you observe. The faster the strobe speed, the better. Even though an ordinary party strobe is helpful, more advanced devices called "stroboscopes" can flash at amazing rates—hundreds of times per second. However, they can be quite expensive, usually running at least $150. Experimenting with different flash rates will ultimately help us learn more about the frequencies and motions of spirits.

Some researchers believe exposure to specific strobe rates exercises the eyes, making them more capable of perceiving certain frequencies of light. In turn, it enhances one's ability to see a ghost. Though the image on your television may seem stable, it actually flickers many times per second. DVDs can produce a different flicker rate than most traditional broadcasts or video, and those who watch DVDs regularly often claim an enhanced ability to see ghosts. This is especially the case when it comes to seeing dark, fleeting entities—called "shadow people"—from the corner of the eye. No one knows who these shadow people are, but seeing ghosts from the corner of the eye is nothing new. Our peripheral vision may even be superior to our straight-ahead vision in some ways. Evolutionarily, that's because in ancient times people needed to see predators creeping up at their sides. Many people claim they can see certain things from the corner of the eye they can't otherwise see. They say various stars are easier to see that way, and in fact, oscillating items, like airplane propellers, are easier to see as well. Just like a strobe light, your brain has a "flicker-fusion" rate. That rate may be different for the peripheral than the forward vision. If so, perhaps that difference is greater for some people than for others.

You should also note that fluorescent lights flicker in relation to their electrical input. In the United States, those plugged into AC outlets flicker 60 times per second. This is in direct relationship to the electricity produced by standard power companies; the AC current switches 120 times per second, or at 60 Hz. Therefore, a fluorescent light is a sort of strobe in and of itself. On some investigations, you may notice more activity beneath their illumination.

TONE GENERATOR

This device is definitely for the advanced ghost researcher. A tone generator is any device that creates sounds at specific hertz. You can search online and find simple, cheap programs that will allow you to generate an infinite range of sounds. A good one can be obtained from NCH Swift Sound by visiting www.nch.com.au or by installing Cool Edit audio software from www.CoolEdit.com.

Some researchers say they've found a correlation between ghost manifestations and "standing waves." Let me explain. When a tone is broadcast in a room, it reflects from its surroundings and ultimately converges at one area where the sound is concentrated. This spot is an invisible pool of energy that forms a pattern, oscillating at a particular, harmonic frequency. We call this a "standing wave." If its frequency is closer to that of a spirit's body, it may indeed affect materialization in some way. These waves can be created by ordinary equipment, like ceiling fans, as well. Any device that produces a sound at regular intervals may produce such a manifestation.

This area of ghost research is highly theoretical. Therefore, as always, you should experiment with it.

FIRST-AID KIT

Ghost hunters often find themselves in secluded areas. Emergency first-aid materials should always be accessible.

BEVERAGE AND SNACK

Ghost hunting can be draining. Be sure not to neglect your basic need for food and liquid. You'll learn more about this necessity in the chapter on conducting investigations.

• • •

Standard human conveniences, like toilet paper, are easy to overlook, but can also be important in the field. Attire should be comfortable, and the more pockets and satchels the better, as you'll have lots to carry. Long hair should be pulled back since it can contaminate a photo or simply fall in one's eyes at an inopportune moment. You'll also want to remember accessories like extension cords or multiple plug-in power strips that may be necessary for some equipment, like video cameras and strobe lights.

As more is learned about ghosts, additional tools will be required to study them effectively. Being mindful of this, you should always be expanding your collection of research instruments. Take what you learn and build on it. Once we finally reach a complete understanding of spirits, we can hope to combine many technologies into one "ghost meter," designed specifically for spectral detection. Form your own theories about the activity, then test them using whatever technology is necessary. This is how virtually all scientific progress is made. You will soon customize your equipment to fit your specific needs. Every ghost hunter's kit is slightly different.

No matter what kind of research technique you use, chances are your results will end up being analyzed on a computer. You can zoom in on photographs and manipulate features that will enhance focus and bring out fine details. You can slow down audio recordings, reverse them, or eliminate distracting hisses, crackles, and pops. You can also plot collected data on spreadsheets, allowing you to produce charts and graphs that illustrate patterns in activity. That being the case, you may also want to consider bringing a laptop with you, if possible. In some cases, it's not necessary to examine results on the spot. At other times, it will be of great benefit.

Having a computer on the scene is not essential, but it might certainly help you maximize the efficiency of your overall investigation. If the computer is online, it will allow you to acquire up-to-date information regarding solar activity and the environment in general.

Much of the equipment you've read about can be purchased at your local shopping mart or electronics store. However, other devices are more rare. The best way to attain those is by doing a search on the Net. This also gives you the opportunity to compare prices from a variety of sources. You might be surprised by the array of devices you can sometimes acquire using auction sites like www.ebay.com. To obtain equipment more easily, please visit my team's web site at www.LEMURteam.com.

THE INVESTIGATION

The number of researchers on your team can be an important element in a ghost investigation. It is valuable to have more than one person. Extra witnesses can help corroborate events, making reported activity more credible. On the other hand, with a smaller number of people, you'll probably have higher chances of experiencing the supernatural. Living human energy might somehow overpower the ghost, making materialization more difficult. Of course, more bodies also add heat and moisture to the air, making it harder to build up charges. If you want to use lots of equipment simultaneously, it may also be necessary to have several people. Whatever the case, a team of ten people is best to research, say, an averaged-sized home. In stark contrast to this, some haunts are most active when lots of people are around. This can be the case especially with hotel ghosts, or entities that choose to reside in socially active places. People lovers in life usually end up being people lovers in the afterlife.

If you want to conduct research all by yourself, the protocol is no different from that for a team. Having a group simply allows you to cover more ground in less time, share and develop ideas, and possibly provide witnesses. Also, ghost research is dependent upon understanding so many kinds of

186 | Joshua P. Warren

subjects (audio, visual, EMF, etc.), and it's almost impossible for one person to be an expert at everything. Instead of juggling everything yourself, it's nice to have knowledgeable individuals who can focus on specific tasks. Regardless of the number of researchers, it always boils down to using the scientific method: observing, collecting, and organizing evidence, then using it to find patterns and correlations, forming hypotheses and theories, and establishing reliable cause and effect.

Even though research data is often thought of as hard and cold, keep in mind that if you visit an occupied haunted house and the spirit is that of a resident's loved one, you must be sensitive to that fact. People often develop relationships with the ghosts that share their homes. Therefore, find out if the specter has a name, and refer to it in a more personal way. This can make the resident feel more comfortable with your presence, and will probably increase your chances of receiving cooperation from the entity. Regardless of the situation, never be afraid to speak out loud to an entity, treating the spirit just like an invisible person in the room. In fact, you can ask them to approach your equipment for documentation, or give you some sign of their presence. Explain who you are, how your equipment works, and what your goal is, then see if it makes a difference.

Following is a synopsis of a typical investigation of an occupied haunted house.

Upon arrival, the crew should meet the owner(s)/resident(s) and make their acquaintance in a general way. Next, a resident usually gives a tour of the grounds. Obviously, you want this tour from the person who has the most knowledge of the grounds and the paranormal activity in question. It's good to see the interior and exterior areas. The more you know about the location, the better. Here are the basic questions to ask:

1. On a timeline, what is the general history of the property?
2. Have any noteworthy or intense events happened here?
3. How long has unexplainable activity been occurring?
4. Are there patterns in the activity?
5. What are possible conventional causes?
6. Are sensitive electronics disrupted on the property (e.g., light bulbs frequently blowing or computers, radios, and TVs working improperly)? This can indicate odd energy fields at work.
7. Do residents of the location experience unusual psychological effects, such as mood swings or strange, vivid dreams? How about physiological? Do residents become tired, sick, or agitated to an extraordinary extent?

During the tour, the resident should recount ghostly experiences and show where they occurred. As the crew observes, they should look for anything in the locations that could provide a conventional explanation for the phenomena. Always remember to rule out ordinary causes before jumping to supernatural conclusions. For example, if strange noises come from the attic, could a tree branch be tapping the house when the wind blows? Are there mice at play? Could a cold spot in the basement be due to a leak in the wall? Are there lots of reflective objects that might cause exceptional reflections in photographs, resembling ghostly images? Use your common sense.

At the close of the tour, it's good to let the resident fill out a standard information form like the one provided at the end of this book. If he or she objects, explain that it's a crucial part of doing thorough research. Such information should be collected from everyone on the scene. Those who have *not* witnessed the supernatural are just as valuable as those who have.

In some cases, you and the location owners may feel more comfortable if each party signs a liability waiver. Such a waiver would release each from responsibility for whatever may happen to the other. For example, if someone with your group falls in the dark and breaks a leg, it would relieve the location owner of responsibility. Or, if you capture a gorgeous ghost photograph, it would prevent the location owner from claiming you didn't have permission to take the photo on his or her property. If you feel it's important to make legal arrangements, consult a lawyer to draw up a simple liability release that basically says everyone will obey the law and one party will not sue the other. Also be sure to include that whatever results you gain legally belong to you. Often, a location owner will want to remain anonymous, so a confidentiality clause can also be included, simply stating that you won't publicize details of the investigation, such as the owner's name or the property's address.

In addition, the research crew should fill out their log for the investigation (see the sample included at the end of this guide). After the forms are completed and the information is assessed and discussed, you should explain to the resident how your equipment works. This usually entails explaining the theoretical basis for ghostly occurrences. You should then give the resident an idea of what you propose to do, and how long it will take to do it. It is important for members of an investigative team to be good communicators. That's because you'll constantly have to explain to residents/owners what you're doing, and make them feel comfortable in such an unusual situation. You should also maintain a sense of humor, helping everyone to relax. Even though death and spirituality are serious subjects, don't forget to have a good time, as long as you're respectful.

Ask if the resident has any special requests (e.g., particular places you should or should not go, or things that you are not welcome to disturb). Remember that although you have passion for your work, that passion does not outrank ownership of the property. Try to be as quiet, respectful, and unobtrusive as possible. You should also inform the resident of any special requests you may have. For example, if you'd like to set up a tape recorder in a room, explain that valid results can be obtained only if the room is left undisturbed. The same would go for trying to capture ghost footprints or almost any form of serious monitoring. With all that said and done, it's good to walk around the location by yourselves, getting a feel for the place. This may also give the entities a chance to get used to you. The crew should discuss anything special that was noticed during this walk-through. A second walk-through should be conducted, this time using handheld tools to get a "primary reading" on the place. This is a general reading to give you a basic idea of where any hot spots may be. Next, the crew should go to the more active areas and try to pinpoint hot spots as specifically as possible. Remember to watch for fields created by artificial means. In more serious investigations, you may want to have a blueprint of the location, to mark areas of bizarre energy.

The crew should decide which areas will be investigated first, and what technology will be designated to those places. A tape recorder may go in one place, a couple with night-vision scopes somewhere else, a couple with dowsing rods somewhere else, and so on. The rest of the time should be spent observing, documenting, and, if desirable, revolving posts. Of course, the specific way in which information is obtained depends upon the purpose of the investigation.

There is no prescriptive set of guidelines for who should go where and what equipment should be used. You simply want to adjust your information gathering to the activity in question. For example, if ghostly noises are frequently heard in the upstairs bathroom, that's a good place to focus your audio recording efforts. Therefore, the person most qualified to handle audio recordings should take that post. If apparitions are most often seen in the living room, that's a great place to set up your cameras with qualified operators. If you are conducting a long-term investigation, you should eventually use each information-gathering tool in every part of the location. Obviously, the more time you can spend at any one spot, the higher your chances of gaining positive results there. However, if you have a limited amount of time (like one night), focus your efforts on the places you're most likely to get results, based upon past reports and primary readings.

Work out a system of marking rooms where equipment is set up to record undisturbed. A piece of red tape on the door will work. Anything that grabs the attention of someone before he or she contaminates an observation area is effective. In addition, each person at the location should be informed of these spots.

Ideally, an investigation should go on all night. Therefore, you may want to have some coffee and snacks on hand. It's always good for researchers to have plenty of beverages. For some reason, investigating haunts commonly dehydrates researchers and drains their energy, perhaps due to the location's tumultuous energies affecting their unadjusted bodies. Of course, that's in addition to the energy it takes to cover lots of ground, if necessary.

Throughout the night, it's best for the residents or owners to do whatever they normally do. They should dine, watch television, shower . . . basically carry on as if the researchers were not present (as much as they can). Their routine may play a role in the supernatural phenomena—especially if some of their activities cue the spirits to behave in a certain way. The residents should also bed down at their normal time.

Most ghost hunters are night owls—people who enjoy being active while the rest of the world is at slumber. However, that's not always the case. The presence of sleeping people may actually aid in ghost materialization. One old theory holds that specters might somehow use the dormant energy of a sleeping person to gain physical power. Some ghost hunters actually bring a "sleeper" along on an investigation. Once at the haunted location, this person's job is to sleep.

By the next morning, ghost hunters who don't sleep are usually worn out. Upon reporting the highlights to the residents, the team usually goes home to sleep. The next day (while events are still fresh on their minds), the crew should regroup and discuss the investigation. A written report, summarizing and detailing activity observed, should be created. A copy of the report goes to the owner(s) and/or resident(s), and a copy is kept for your research file, complete with support materials like photos, video footage, or other evidence. Of course, if significant activity was observed, this usually leads to further investigation.

Step-by-step, you should:

1. Learn the general history and layout of the location.
2. Take care of paperwork like interview forms and preparing data logs.
3. Locate hot spots by taking primary readings.
4. Document as much information as possible about each environment present.

5. Review results, looking for correlations and patterns.
6. Rule out conventional phenomena, leaving only anomalous activity.

Each time you return to that location, you should narrow your search based upon the last investigation's results. This will maintain your efficiency, enabling you to use your limited resources studying the most worthy, anomalous phenomena.

It is important to realize that each ghost investigation is different. The variables are always changing. All in all, the procedure is based primarily on common sense. As long as you have good documentation of the setting and events, you'll probably be fine. Again, the method of operation is always structured in relation to what you want to achieve. An excursion to merely document specters would be viewed differently from one to clear a location of spirits. Define what you intend to do, then build your procedure around accomplishing that specific goal.

Many ghost hunters wonder if it's ethical to charge for their services. After all, there are people who are willing to pay for a good investigation. Is it wrong to accept their money? I have devoted thousands of dollars and many years of my life to this field. I find it almost insulting when someone says I don't deserve to be compensated for my time and experience. There are some ignorant critics who imply that a paid person cannot be an honest person. However, every other type of researcher gets paid. No one criticizes biologists, chemists, astronomers, or physicists for being compensated. Your doctor charges for each visit, but does that mean his service is not legitimate? What is your job? Would you perform it better if you weren't being paid? It is ludicrous to think that a paranormal researcher automatically undermines his or her credibility by accepting money. We pay our bills just like everyone else. In fact, it is essential to earn money if high tech research is to progress. Of course, regardless of the profession, it *is* a problem if the payment influences the integrity of the work. When conducting an investigation, paid or not, you must offer only HONEST results: that's the closest thing to a paranormal researcher's Hippocratic Oath. Do not feel bad about accepting money, as long as it is honestly earned and deserved.

WHEN YOU FIND THEM . . .

Lots of people are so preoccupied with finding ghosts that they don't prepare for what to do *when* they find them. If you just want to catch a glimpse of one, that's fine. However, if you want more, you must have the means necessary to approach your goal. Aside from documenting them and the conditions of their materialization, you may want to communicate with them, or even get rid of them. If that's the case, you're stepping into a whole new arena.

Aside from documenting your experience with all available means, there is no standard procedure for what to do when you encounter a ghost. As is usually the case, it all depends on your individual reasons for exploring the activity. Whatever the case, if you encounter an unfamiliar entity, treat it just like a stranger on the street: with common courtesy and respect. Remember that most entities are simply humans in a different form.

COMMUNICATION WITH SPIRITS

When Franklin D. Roosevelt was in office, the queen of the Netherlands tried to interest his wife, Eleanor, in spiritual communication. Upon hearing the pitch, Mrs. Roosevelt replied, "Since we're going to be dead such a long time anyway, it's rather a waste of time chatting with all of them before we get there." For most people, that seems to be a logical perspective. Of course, not everyone feels that way.

Let's be realistic. There is no reliable way to communicate with spirits. If there were, there would be no controversy over the existence of an afterlife. However, that doesn't mean you can't experiment. Test different methods to develop your own opinions about spiritual communication. Following are a few common techniques you may want to explore.

Psychics

The oldest way of attempting spiritual communication is through the use of mediums. This is also the most unreliable. Since biblical times, mediums have attempted to speak with the dead using special psychic abilities. Although everyone possesses some psychic ability, many professional psychics are frauds. Genuine psychic ability is usually sporadic. There are *some* people who are genuine, though. Those are the truly gifted.

For centuries, and especially in the 1800s, mediums have held séances attempting to communicate with spirits. At these sessions, bells ring, objects move, and all manner of bizarre things can manifest. However, it's usually just a clever show. Harry Houdini was so disgusted with mediums that he devoted a good portion of his life to disproving them. Such sessions were usually held to cash in on a grieving person's need to have final communication with a lost loved one. The worst thing about séances was that they damaged the public's view of spiritualism. Because of the unscrupulous activity, many believed (and still do) that all ghostly activity was fraudulent. This is similar to how fake spirit photography damaged the field as well.

The worst thing about utilizing psychics for ghost detection is that *you're using one unexplained phenomenon to try to explain another.* There is no universally accepted proof that psychic ability exists. Therefore, why should you think it will help you make a case for ghostly activity? If you must bring a psychic onto the scene, do not give him or her any information about the haunting. Receive feedback, and then decide whether or not it will help lead you in a direction that can be confirmed using scientific methods.

A legitimate psychic can be truly valuable to an investigation. Even though the instruments are essential for solidifying objective facts, they cannot give you names and ages of spirits, or illustrate historical scenarios pertinent to a ghost. If a psychic is genuine, he or she might be able to color your data with more emotional substance. Whatever the case, a genuine psychic should not be offended by your skepticism of his or her abilities. Make the psychic prove it. A fraudulent psychic is a waste of your time. At least a professional magician is entertaining.

Aside from enlisting psychic power, there *is* a way you can sometimes use your body as a ghost detector. Humans can easily feel electrostatic fields. Place your hand an inch in front of your television. The thick static field will press softly against your flesh, making the hair on your hand stand on end. If you are especially sensitive to this feeling, try walking around a haunted area with your arms and palms outstretched. Be intimately cognizant of what you feel. If your hands pass through a strong electrostatic field, it will feel like your television screen. People vary in their sensitivity to this sensation.

Some are so sensitive to ghostly energies that they can't tolerate them. It's not uncommon for people to become nauseated in the presence of a haunted place. A couple of years ago, I visited a glorious three-story house that had only one active room: a spacious bedroom on the top floor. It was visually spectacular; however, the woman who owned the house could not enter that room. After only ten or fifteen seconds, she would begin to feel extremely sick. That was the only strange phenomenon she personally experienced, even though other members of the household had seen apparitions on the floor. No one else felt nauseated in the room. It apparently had to do with her individual sensitivity.

It seems children can be especially keen. In fact, children may have a better ability to experience ghosts in general, possibly because they are not using their brain power to focus on the daily distractions of adulthood. I investigated one haunted house inhabited by a family with an eight-year-old girl. She slept by herself in an upstairs bedroom. After the family had lived there a week, the girl began telling her father about a cowboy she'd seen walking into an unoccupied room across the hall. The figure would step into the room and vanish. Having seen nothing unusual himself, the father ignored the tales as childhood fancy until a neighbor told him of a man who'd killed himself in that bedroom in the 1930s. Of course, men in that day often wore hats. A child might easily perceive such a figure as a cowboy.

Ouija Boards

Ouija boards have become one of the most popular devices for communicating with the dead. They consist simply of a board upon which an alphabet and numbers are printed. Two users, usually male and female, lightly rest their fingers on a pointer. Then, questions are presented to whatever spirits may be in the area. Supposedly, the pointer begins to slide around the board, spelling out answers. There are many rumors about Ouija boards. Some claim only evil spirits can be contacted with them. Others say you should never use one alone, or you might be overpowered and possessed by a malign entity.

Despite all the hoopla, there is very little evidence that Ouija boards work at all. In many cases, one user is trying to trick the other by manipulating the pointer. But the most common influence on their behavior is called "automatism." This is a process by which the human brain subconsciously manipulates nerve impulses and tiny muscular contractions to cause an involuntary motion. For example, take an unlatched necklace and let it dangle from your fingertips. Then vividly imagine the necklace swinging in a clockwise circle. After a few moments, the necklace *will* begin to swing in a clockwise circle, though you're not trying to do it. You can then imagine it swinging in a counterclockwise circle, or back and forth, or side to side. In any case, the necklace will respond, swinging in the manner in which it's visualized. The mere visualization makes the body subconsciously respond. If you didn't know better, you'd think it was telekinesis. If you have preconceived notions about an answer on a Ouija board, you may subconsciously influence it.

It is possible that a Ouija board may sometimes function as a "psionic device." This is an instrument that one uses to directly access his or her psychic ability. Though we each probably have some psychic ability, physically oriented society tries to make us believe we do not. This self-doubt may prevent us from accessing our abilities by convincing us that they do not exist. However, we can use a tool to access this potential. Living in a physical world, we naturally place more faith in physical things. It's possible that a Ouija board could serve as a tool to access your inherent ESP. Though you may be consciously unaware of the process, automatism may move the device by tapping in to your psychic mind. In this manner, answers are coming from yourself, but you don't realize it.

However Ouija boards may or may not work, some people swear by them. As with all things, I suggest you experiment. Then you can decide if a Ouija board works for you.

Automatic Writing

Automatic writing is another example of using a psionic device. In this case, the instruments are a simple pad and pencil or pen. A subject takes the writing implement, places it on the paper, then lets his or her mind wander. After a few minutes, the hand begins to doodle. It is important for the subject *not* to pay attention to what the hand is writing. In some cases, intelligent phrases are written. Oftentimes, messages from the spirit world are reportedly received—especially if this is the realm the subject is trying to access.

Automatic writing *can* be used in a more specific way. The process is most commonly used by those trying to tap in to their subconscious minds to explain their neuroses and phobias. For example, one might ask: "Why am I afraid of snakes?" Then, the mind is allowed to wander. Sometimes a response or image will be written or drawn that helps answer the question. Finding the source of a problem is the first step to remedying it.

The problem with this method lies in the operation of the mind. The human subconscious is a jumbled, vast, and confusing place. When using automatic writing to communicate with the dead, you can hardly ever be sure if responses come from the spirit world or inside yourself.

The Pendulum

Another psionic device that is popular for phantasmal communication is the pendulum. You can make a pendulum from a length of string or fishing line, perhaps six to ten inches long, attached to a small weight. A lead fishing weight actually works quite well. The more balanced the weight, the better. Therefore, a symmetrically shaped object is advised.

You next draw a circle (perhaps the size of a fifty-cent piece) on paper. Within this circle, draw a cross. The resulting image looks like crosshairs. Lay the paper on a table. Then, hold the pendulum directly over the diagram, an inch or so above, resting your elbow on the table (Illus. 28). You must next designate one swinging direction (back and forth) as "yes." The other would then become "no." Instead of using back and forth, you can also use clockwise and counterclockwise.

With this setup, you can ask a spirit questions at any haunted location. Of course, the inquiries should be phrased so that a "yes" or "no" response would answer them. Upon

28. A pendulum in use over a crosshair design. *Photo courtesy Joshua P. Warren*

asking a question, the pendulum should begin to move accordingly. Holding the device over the cross helps to see the direction in which it's moving. As with the Ouija board, the downfall to this technique is automatism. It is very easy for the user to subconsciously influence the pendulum's motions by anticipating a response. As with similar methods, its answers should be taken lightly.

These are a few of the most common means of attempting to communicate with the spirit world. The list can go on and on. There have even been some inventors who have devoted years to building complicated devices that would allow humans to speak with the dead. Thomas Edison himself worked on one! But I must reiterate, there are *no* reliable means of doing so. Until a dependable method is invented, you should focus more on objective ways of documenting phantoms. Subjective techniques only muddle the process and usually turn out to be counterproductive.

CLEARING A LOCATION OF ACTIVITY

Most people who own or live in haunted places are not particularly bothered by it. As long as most of the activity is innocent, it is viewed as a curious stimulant for novel conversation. However, sometimes a person will want the presence to leave. Dreary spirits can make a place seem melancholy and depressing, taking a toll on the residents. Malicious ones might be downright cruel. Though the roles of ghost researcher and exorcist are not the same, you can offer *some* assistance.

The most common way to clear a location of an entity is simply by asking, or commanding, the entity to leave. This might seem like a naïve way of approaching the situation.

However, it often works. Apparently, many specters do stick around by choice. In order to make the process more effective, it's most often done in a ritualistic way.

A ceremony is a way of formally solidifying intents and occasions. Think about how we usually incorporate them into society. One of the most common is a wedding ceremony. The ceremony is completely unnecessary. Couples can simply go fill out a form and be done. However, the paperwork serves only the legal end. Isn't there more to marriage than mere legalities? Marriage ceremonies are designed to focus on a singular intent: bringing two people together for life. Those of importance are asked to be there to witness the occasion and to contribute their minds and souls to the event. There is nothing vague or wishy-washy about it. Everything is made clear and public. The symbols of marriage—the rings—have meaning, but only because we apply meaning to them. The entire occasion is a symbolic way of stating a situation. Symbols are only as good as the meaning we give them. If our thoughts were not actively important, we wouldn't have symbols.

Asking an entity to leave in a ceremonial way is equally important because it demonstrates the seriousness of the intentions. Such a ritual usually entails you, your colleagues, and the property owners or residents sitting down together in a peaceful, quiet environment. At that point, you might want to burn candles and incense or do whatever will represent cleansing in the mind of the property owners. Establishing a strong proprietary sense in the owner always helps. This person must be consciously aware that he or she controls the location, and this should help add strength to his resolution.

Utilizing the owner's belief system is also a powerful tool. It can make him or her feel more comfortable and give him a familiar avenue by which to access his spiritual strength. For example, a Catholic may sprinkle an area with holy water. In any case, physical actions represent mental intent, and mental intent is what ultimately does the work. It's all a fancy way of firmly and officially asking the presence to leave. This might be all it takes.

There are individuals who seem to command more respect from spirits. These people have a higher rate of success when asking ghosts to leave. Regardless of religious affiliation or other such variables, it seems these people simply make a greater impact on the physical environment. Such a gift is a mystery. However, those in desperate situations may want to seek this type of individual. The best way is by conducting a search online or visiting www.LEMURteam.com for an up-to-date referral.

If you get the feeling that a haunting entity wants to accomplish a specific goal, you might also end the activity by helping it achieve that goal. This relates to the unfinished-business category. If the spirit wants to identify a murderer, offer a goodbye, unveil a hidden treasure, or anything else of this nature, you might find a way to assist. Does the activity point in a certain direction? Do you find consistent clues or patterns? If ghostly activity displays a common theme, follow up on that theme. Maybe a hammer falls off a shelf frequently. Is someone in the family a carpenter? Is something important placed within a nailed-shut box? Don't overlook the forest for the trees. What might a ghost be trying to tell you?

One past associate of mine began experiencing an array of ghostly activity and negative synchronicity after a trip to France. Being a meticulous fellow, he carefully noted the occurrences and realized that they most often took place in proximity to a souvenir from his vacation. While exploring the catacombs below Paris on Bastille Day, he'd pulled a tooth from a skull and kept it as a memento. Upon realizing its connection to the disturbing activity, he promptly took it to a cemetery and buried it respectfully. The ghostly occurrences stopped at once. Apparently, the spirit only wanted its remains to rest in peace.

On the other hand, at an indoor locale, there *is* a more scientific way of dealing with the problem. If it is true that ghostly interaction with the physical world is dependent upon manipulation of electrical ions, you can control the amount of these available. To enhance ghostly activity, you want the environment to be dry. Therefore, you can run a dehumidifier to increase spectral phenomena. By the same token, you can do just the opposite to hinder such activity. Running a humidifier in an area adds moisture to the air. This makes charges leak away. If you keep a humidifier running, it should greatly decrease the ghostly activity in a haunted indoor area.

I once investigated a location where the owners, a husband and wife, were being plagued by malevolent activity. Sometimes, as they'd walk down a particular hallway, an icy hand would slap their faces. They were afraid of sleeping at night because they'd sometimes wake up to find the phantom, a man glowing blue—his face menacing—hovering over their bed. On one occasion, the husband almost had a heart attack upon waking up to the chilling sight. They were ready to move, and they called me as a last resort. These people had already asked the entity to leave on several occasions, and had even brought in priests and ministers to bless the grounds, all to no avail. Upon locating three paranormal hot spots in the house, I suggested they place a humidifier at each location, running twenty-four hours a day. They complied, and within two days the activity ceased.

Throughout the years, I've seen this simple solution help many people. However, the humidifiers must be placed at the correct areas—those spots where the spirit seems to be gaining its energy. On the other hand, there have also been many cases in which the humidifiers did not work. It seems that altering the physical environment interferes only with a spirit's ability to materialize electrically. Also, the effectiveness may be restricted to the strength and mastery of an entity. However, imprints can frequently be terminated in this way.

Sprinkling salt around the grounds is also said to be beneficial in some cases. Salt is composed of crystals, and these structures manipulate the energy environment, sometimes neutralizing the necessary conditions for paranormal activity. Salt can also symbolize cleansing: absorbing the activity just like it absorbs water.

Earlier, we discussed the significance of mirrors as well. If you find ghostly activity taking place around mirrors, try altering their position. This is especially so if you find two mirrors facing each other. Something so simple can end the activity in some cases.

Ultimately, as with communication, there is no guaranteed way to rid a location of all entities. Unfortunately, we don't have a trap like the one used in the movie *Ghostbusters*—a device that will suck a ghost into a box for safekeeping. This is a testament to how little we actually understand about how spirits function in the physical world. But that's why it's so important to scientifically document their presence and behavior as much as possible. If we do so effectively, we should eventually be able to find a way of controlling them. As it is, many residents of haunted houses simply have to bite the bullet and move.

PROTECTING YOURSELF
FROM GHOSTS

Novice ghost hunters are commonly concerned about the hazards of seeking the supernatural. The greatest threat is their own psychological weakness. Desiring to come face-to-face with an entity is one thing. Doing it is quite another. There is usually nothing to fear. Most ghosts do not have the power or will to do serious physical harm. But humans have a natural fear of the unknown, and ghosts embody that morbid fear. Someone who is not prepared to experience a spectral encounter may have a heart attack when, and if, it happens. This is especially the case if that person is alone when it happens. For that reason, it is important to be psychologically prepared.

On the Fourth of July, 2001, a hotel in the southeastern United States held a spectacular fireworks show. In the middle of the display, a security guard was checking an old building on the property, all by himself. He turned a corner and was surprised to see a man, wearing a derby, standing in a darkened room. His back was to the guard as he stared out a grand bay window, apparently enjoying the fireworks. The guard called to him and the man turned, gave a blank stare, then disappeared. When the guard burst back into headquarters, he was sobbing like a baby. The experience had undermined his entire concept of reality. He quit his job due to the encounter.

The security guard was totally unprepared for a blatant run-in with the paranormal. Currently, I'm told, he's the co-warden of a prison. This is obviously a man who isn't afraid of any physical foe. However, a completely harmless paranormal experience caused him an enormous amount of psychological shock. There are ways to help you prepare for this shock, though.

Some ghost hunters enact a psychic self-defense technique before entering the grounds of a potentially negative spirit. This entails imagining one's body surrounded by a shield of protective white light. Formed by thought, this shield may be nonphysical—but then, so are ghosts. Such psychic barriers may help by focusing the individual's mental strength.

Other ghost hunters conduct a ritual consistent with their belief system. For example, a prayer might be uttered before entering haunted grounds. Carrying items of faith, such as crosses and Bibles, is also commonplace. Anything that symbolizes the individual's mental and spiritual strength can be beneficial. Do whatever makes you feel more comfortable.

Novice ghost hunters also wonder if specters can follow them home. This rarely happens. But in those cases where it does happen, the individual must verbally command the spirit to leave his or her home. Being a physical creature, you can assert your dominance over the physical world. Your mental strength can drive a ghost away. Usually, those who suffer from spiritual intrusions are too psychologically weak to stand up to spirits. On the nonphysical plane, thoughts can be weapons. Use yours effectively.

Aside from psychological threats, there is indeed a physical one. I have seen physical objects being manipulated by unseen forces on numerous occasions. The largest of these was a meter that weighed slightly less than a pound. It was during a L.E.M.U.R. investigation, and Brian Irish captured the incident on video. The meter squealed with energy readings as it was knocked forward, then up on its side. Less than a pound may not sound too intimidating. However, a stronger spirit should be able to move more. A vase flying off a top shelf could do some painful damage to your head. There's not much you can do about this kind of risk except to be aware of your surroundings. If you're in an area where objects could present a danger, especially if they're unstably positioned to begin with, exercise caution.

Also, the presence of a ghost can sometimes blow light bulbs. An entire series of bulbs can go, marking the spirit's path of travel. This may be an indication of the specter's powerful energy overwhelming the delicate filament. In rarer cases, the bulbs actually explode. Obviously, this can present a formidable danger. I've even seen lamps that spontaneously caught fire due to this phenomenon. In fact, at extreme locations, mechanical and electrical devices can be caused to combust on a regular basis.

The chance of being physically attacked by an entity is extremely low. Those instances are so few and far between that you'll probably never encounter it, unless you become a prolific ghost researcher. A physical touch is far more common, but an attack, in which undeniable harm was intended, is certainly an oddity among oddities. It's even more rare to hear of someone being raped or molested by an entity. In fact, those cases are so exceptional that no thorough study of the phenomenon has been conducted. The most famous episode of this activity is a case that was made into a 1982 movie called *The Entity*, starring Barbara Hershey.

Of course, everyone also wonders about this thing called "possession." Is it possible for a spirit to enter your body and control your actions? I have researched numerous reports of people who claim to be possessed, and have witnessed several exorcisms. In each case, the individual claimed that the presence filled them with dread and depression, injecting thoughts of suicide or the will to harm others. During exorcisms, I've seen people grunt and groan for hours, frowning as if in agony. I've heard unfamiliar sounds and languages roll from their tongues, and seen their bodies swell with unbridled emotion. However, I've never seen anything that couldn't have been the product of a good acting job. That's not to say there was no authenticity to the experience, but that there was no objective evidence to suggest the person was actually being possessed. And I've definitely never seen a head spin around and vomit pea soup!

At the same time, I have certainly seen people's personalities change, over a period of time, upon moving into haunted houses or coming into extended contact with active locations. For example, if someone moves into a home that's haunted by the ghost of a drunkard, that person may gradually become an alcoholic. I have also seen people become happier individuals when the spirit is a positive influence. I'm not sure whether you'd call this true possession, or just someone being swayed by his or her surroundings. If you hang out with criminals, you're liable to become a criminal. If you hang out with fishermen, you're liable to end up going fishing. It's only natural for people to be influenced by those around them. Why should it be any different if those influences come from spirits?

If an entity draws a person's energy long enough, it may also decrease that individual's resistance to sickness. Illnesses can be greatly enhanced at hauntings. In the worst-case scenarios, like those presented by the infamous Bell Witch episode of Adams, Tennessee, someone can die from this. In the early 1800s, the Bell Witch was an evil spirit that apparently tormented a man, John Bell, to death. He suffered from a series of mysterious ailments and bizarre physical manifestations (like a painful swollen tongue) until he died.

EPILOGUE

By now, you should have a solid foundation in the basic theories and techniques that drive current ghost hunters. Of course, no one knows for certain how ghostly activity functions. That is what makes paranormal research so exciting, though. Because of this, anyone's views are conceptually as good as anyone else's. There is plenty of room for all perspectives, opinions, and ideas. The world of the unknown is a creative place. Its lack of definition provides the blank slate upon which we can draw our own designs. Ultimately, the truth will bubble to the surface, as it always does. By testing every theory and hypothesis, we can at least rule out the things that prove ineffective. Elimination is an important key to discovery.

For at least thousands of years, humans have tried to discover a direct way to access the spiritual realm. Many believe that such an advance will never happen. However, for thousands of years humans tried to invent a flying machine. It was thought to be as impossible as ever when the Wright brothers revolutionized the world. Many researchers prefer to study things already discovered, while others crave the thrill of the discovery itself. Paranormal investigators must thrive on the excitement inspired by the brink of discovery—delving into that vast unknown realm that looms about our familiar, routine lives. The unknown is the breeding ground of hope and freedom. It alone shelters every profound development our future will bring.

As you investigate this vast universe, I hope you will approach each scenario respectfully. We're all in the same boat—trying simply to survive and to understand our purpose. Life will treat you the way you treat it, and you must approach each day with an open mind and a hungry heart. Never pretend to know all the answers. All the answers are not known. Whether in nature or human society, the world of our senses is an illusion; you must look below the surface to find the ultimate truth. There are many who would rather explain away life's mysteries with unfounded conjecture than accept a complex reality for what it truly is. I trust you will not be that kind of person. Instead, I hope you will be an *explorer.*

Though this guide touches only the broad surface of ghost research, you should now be prepared to start studying the spectral world. By learning about the afterlife, we will benefit this life invaluably. There are lots of ghosts, and every contributing mind is precious.

As the visible world is sustained by the invisible, so men, through all their trials and sins and sordid vocations, are nourished by the beautiful visions of their solitary dreamers.
—James Allen, *As a Man Thinketh*

APPENDIX I

GHOST RESEARCH LOG

Date: _____

Your name: _____

Location name: _____

Address of location: _____

_____

Investigators present: _____

_____

Goal of investigation: _____

Equipment (circle):

Meters   Temp. gauge   Dowsing tools   Night vision
Still camera   Audio enhancer   Audio recorder
Electrostatic generator
Strobe light   Other _____

Type of photography (circle): Standard color
Standard b&w   Infrared   Ultraviolet

Type of film (circle): 35mm   Polaroid   Digital   Other _____

Type of video (circle): VHS   S-VHS   Hi-8   Betacam SP
Digital   Other _____

Type of audio recorder (circle): Analog tape Digital

Type of electrostatic/electromagnetic generator (circle):

Wimshurst   Van de Graaff   Tesla coil   Other _____

Owner of location: _____

Telephone number of owner: _____

Does this location have structures? (circle):   Yes   No

If so, how many?: _____

What are the structures?: _____

What is the oldest
structure?: _____

What year was it
built?: _____

Is the location occupied? (circle):   Yes   No

How many
occupants?: _____

Notable
History: _____

Significant Phenomena Observed on Investigation:

Time: Observer(s)/Phenomena

_____   _____

_____   _____

_____   _____

_____   _____

_____   _____

_____   _____

_____   _____

_____   _____

_____   _____

_____   _____

_____   _____

_____   _____

_____   _____

_____   _____

_____   _____

_____   _____

_____   _____

_____   _____

APPENDIX II

INTERVIEW FORM FOR OWNER/RESIDENT

Name: _____

I am the (circle): Owner   Resident   Other_____

Address of location: _____

_____

My telephone number: _____

Number of residents: _____

Names & ages of other residents: _____

_____

How long have you lived here?: _____

Your occupation: _____

Your age: _____ (optional)

What year was the oldest structure here built?: _____

Has anyone ever died or been killed here? (circle):
Yes   No   Don't know

Explain:

_____

_____

_____

General history of location: _____

_____

_____

Do you believe in ghosts? (circle):   Yes   No   Undecided

Do you believe in psychic phenomena? (circle):   Yes   No   Undecided

Did you ever have a ghostly experience before coming here? (circle):
Yes   No   Don't know

Explain: _____

_____

_____

_____

Have you experienced strange or unexplainable phenomena here?
(circle):   Yes   No

If so, how many times: _____

Explain: _____

_____

_____

_____

_____

_____

_____

_____

_____

_____

_____

_____

_____

_____

EQUIPMENT RESOURCES

Throughout the text, references to various equipment suppliers were given. Here is complete supplier information for some of the most rare or essential tools.

ELECTROMAGNETIC FIELD METERS

Less EMF, Inc.
26 Valley View Lane
Ghent, NY 12075
(888) LESS-EMF
www.lessEMF.com

DIGITAL STILL AND VIDEO CAMERAS

Sony Electronics, Inc.
680 Kinderkamack Road
Oradell, NJ 07649
(800) 222-7669
www.sony.com

AUDIO ENHANCING TECHNOLOGY

Silver Creek Industries, Inc.
P.O. Box 1988

1909 Silver Creek Road
Manitowoc, WI 54221
(800) 533-3277
www.SilverCreekIndustries.com

ELECTROSTATIC GENERATORS

Edmund Scientific
60 Pearce Ave.
Tonawanda, NY 14150-6711
(800) 728-6999
www.ScientificsOnline.com

For more information, visit: www.LEMURteam.com

GLOSSARY OF PARANORMAL TERMS

Apparition—the visible form of a ghost.

Anniversary Imprint—an imprint that usually manifests around the same time each year.

Astral Projection—the conscious initiation of an out-of-body experience.

Aura—a field of energy that emanates from matter. It is especially prominent around living things. Some claim to see it as various colors.

Automatic Writing—expressing subconscious thoughts or influences by doodling.

Chi—Asian term for a "life force" or biological energy that is inhaled and can be manipulated for specific purposes (also called ki).

Clairvoyance—the ability to obtain knowledge based on unexplainable intuition, vision, or various psychic senses.

Clearing—ridding a location of ghostly activity.

Cold Spots—self-contained patches of cool air strewn about haunted locations. They may be ghosts that cannot fully materialize.

Doppelganger—a ghost of the present that looks identical to a living person but behaves differently.

Double—a ghost of the present that looks and behaves identically to a living person.

Dowsing—interpreting the motions of rods, sticks, pendulums, and other such instruments to obtain information (also called divining).

Ectoplasm—any physical substance created by, or accompanying, a spirit's materialization.

Electromagnetic Energy—a hybrid of electrical charges and magnetic fields that binds nature.

Entity—a conscious, interactive ghost.

ESP—acronym for "extrasensory perception"; obtaining information from a source other than the five physical senses (i.e., sight, smell, hearing, taste, touch).

Etheric Body—a layer of the physical body, mimicking its design, but composed entirely of energy.

EVP—acronym for "electronic voice phenomena"; capturing ghostly sounds and/or words on an audio recording.

Exorcism—ridding a person or a location of evil spirits by using religious rites.

Ghost—some paranormal aspect of the physical form and/or mental presence that appears to exist apart from the original physical form.

Ghost Hunter—one who seeks to experience and document ghostly activity.

Harbinger—a ghost of the future that brings warning of impending events.

Haunted Location—an area where ghostly activity occurs regularly, especially for more than a year. Some researchers refer to locations plagued by imprints only as "haunted."

Hot Spot—a site within a haunted location where activity is prominent and/or energy fields are focused.

Imprint—ghostly activity that appears nonconscious and redundant.

Ion—an electrically charged atom or molecule.

Magnetosphere—the magnetic field surrounding the earth.

Materialization—the process by which a spirit creates a physical representation of itself in the physical world.

Medium—one who claims to possess an ability to communicate with spirits.

Natural—a rare phenomenon that appears ghostly but in fact is created by some scientifically unknown property of the present nature.

Necromancy—interacting with the dead, particularly for the purpose of communication or resurrection.

Original Momentum—the initial force or energy necessary to create motion telekinetically.

Out-of-Body Experience—when one's consciousness exits the restrictions of the physical body (also called OBE).

Paranormal Research—the study of phenomena currently considered unexplainable by the mainstream sciences.

PK—acronym for "psychokineses" (see Telekinesis).

Poltergeist—German for "noisy ghost"; an entity or energy that displays sensational interaction with the physical environment, and manifests only when a specific individual or individuals are present.

Portal—a theoretical doorway of energy, through which spirits may be able to enter or exit a location.

Possession—the act of being physically or mentally controlled by spiritual forces, usually negative.

Precognition—seeing or knowing activity received from the future using ESP.

Premonition—a psychic awareness of future events, often with a negative outcome.

Primary Readings—the initial measurements of energy taken at a haunted location, used for establishing an investigation's direction.

Psi—a general, all-encompassing term for "psychic phenomena."

Psionics—the use of physical tools to assist in accessing or interpreting one's ESP.

Psychic—phenomena rooted in ESP and spiritualism; also, a person gifted with ESP.

Retrocognition—seeing or knowing activity from the past using ESP.

Revenant—an entity that comes back only a few times after death.

Séance—a ritual held to communicate with spirits of the dead.

Spiritualism—belief in a spiritual world and/or the ability to communicate with spirits of the dead.

Synchronicity—the product of numerous, seemingly unrelated variables joining to create a common event or remarkable "coincidence."

Telepathy—the process by which a mind can communicate directly with another without using normal, physical interaction or ordinary sensory perception.

Telekinesis—the ability to control one's physical environment without using physical manipulation or force (also known as psychokinesis, TK, or PK).

Warp—a location where the known laws of physics do not always apply and space/time may be distorted.

BIBLIOGRAPHY

Andrews, Ted. *How to See and Read the Aura.* St. Paul, MN: Llewellyn Publications, 1991.

Auerbach, Loyd. *ESP, Hauntings and Poltergeists: A Parapsychologist's Handbook.* New York: Warner Books, 1986.

——. *Mind Over Matter.* New York: Kensington Books, 1996.

Becker, Robert O., M.D., and Gary Seldon. *The Body Electric: Electromagnetism and the Foundation of Life.* New York: William Morrow & Co., Inc., 1985.

Cohen, Daniel. *The Encyclopedia of Ghosts.* New York: Avon Books, 1984.

Cosimano, Charles W. *Psychic Power.* St. Paul, MN: Llewellyn Publications, 1987.

——. *Psionic Power.* St. Paul, MN: Llewellyn Publications, 1989.

Evans, Hilary, and Patrick Huyghe. *The Field Guide to Ghosts and Other Apparitions.* New York: Quill, 2000.

Eysenck, Hans J., and Carl Sargent. *Explaining the Unexplained: Mysteries of the Paranormal.* London: PRION, 1993.

Haining, Peter. *A Dictionary of Ghosts.* Great Britain: Robert Hale, Ltd., 1982.

Halverson, William H. *A Concise Introduction to Philosophy.* New York: McGraw-Hill, Inc., 1981.

Harth, Erich. *Windows on the Mind.* New York: William Morrow & Co., Inc., 1982.

Klein, Aaron E. *Beyond Time and Matter.* New York: Doubleday & Company, Inc., 1973.

LeCron, Leslie M. *Self-Hypnotism.* New York: Signet, 1964.

Lindgren, Dr. C. E. "Capturing Your Aura on Film." *FATE* (January 1995): 32.

Maurey, Eugene. *Exorcism.* West Chester, Pennsylvania: Whitford Press, 1988.

Pearce, Q. L., and Phyllis Emert. *50 Scariest Places and Strangest Mysteries.* New York: Barnes & Noble, 1995.

Psychic Powers (Mysteries of the Unknown). Richmond, Virginia: Time-Life Books, 1987.

Sagan, Carl. *The Demon-Haunted World.* New York: Ballantine Books, 1996.

Sheldrake, Rupert. *Seven Experiments That Could Change the World.* New York: Riverhead Books, 1995.

Warren, Joshua P. *Haunted Asheville.* Asheville, North Carolina: Shadowbox Publications, 1996.

INDEX

ABOUT THE AUTHOR

Joshua P. Warren was born in Asheville, North Carolina, and has lived in the Blue Ridge Mountains his entire life. At the age of thirteen, he wrote his first published book. Since then, he has published numerous titles including *Haunted Asheville, The Evil in Asheville,* and *The Lonely Ameba.* Warren is also the president of his multimedia productions company, Shadowbox Enterprises, LLC. His articles have been published internationally, and he or his work has been featured in such mainstream periodicals as *Southern Living, Delta Sky, FATE,* and *Something About the Author.* A winner of the University of North Carolina Thomas Wolfe Award for Fiction, he wrote columns and articles for the *Asheville Citizen-Times* from 1992 to 1995.

A widely consulted expert on paranormal research, he was hired by the famous Grove Park Inn Resort and Spa to be the first person to officially investigate the Pink Lady apparition in 1995. He also led the expedition that captured the first known footage of the Brown Mountain Lights in 2000. Such work has earned the attention of The Discovery Channel, The Travel Channel, and the NPR, CNN, ABC, CBS and NBC networks and/or affiliates. He is frequently asked to be a guest on radio shows across North America, including

Coast to Coast A.M. with Art Bell. He is the founder and president of L.E.M.U.R., an active paranormal research team based in Asheville, and each year he produces and hosts an interactive Paranormal Conference at the historic Grove Park Inn.

Warren is also an international-award-winning filmmaker, having worked on the sets of numerous films including Warner Brothers' *My Fellow Americans*, Universal's *Patch Adams, Paradise Falls*, and the comedy *Inbred Rednecks*. You may contact him through www.ShadowboxENT.com or www.LEMURteam.com.